HOME SEWN

Cassandra Ellis is a designer of contemporary homewares and patterns, as well as an author and interiors stylist. Originally from New Zealand, Cassandra now runs her own London-based design studio. As well as a pattern and homewares store, Cassandra works directly with clients on commissions, writing, styling and interiors projects as well as running workshops from her London studio. She is the author of three other books – *Quilt Love* (2012), *Cloth* (2013) and *World of Quilts* (2014). Cassandra's work has been featured in *Elle Decoration, House & Garden, Homes & Garden, Red, The Simple Life* and *Mollie Makes*. She has been profiled in the national press by *The Times*, the *Telegraph* and the *Guardian*.

CASSANDRA ELLIS

HOME SEWN

over 30 contemporary cushions, curtains, quilts & more

photography by Catherine Gratwicke

Kyle Books

First published in Great Britain in 2015 by Kyle Books,
an imprint of Kyle Cathie Ltd
192-198 Vauxhall Bridge Road
London SW1V 1DX
general.enquiries@kylebooks.com
www.kylebooks.com

10 9 8 7 6 5 4 3 2 1

ISBN 978 0 85783 162 0

Editor: Vicky Orchard
Designer: Miranda Harvey
Photographer: Catherine Gratwicke
Styling: Cassandra Ellis
Illustrations: Grace Helmer
Production: Lisa Pinnell

A Cataloguing in Publication record
for this title is available from the
British Library.

Colour reproduction by ALTA London
Printed and bound in Singapore by Tien
Wah Press

For Beryl and Suzie

contents

introduction

When I started planning *Home Sewn* my starting point was my own home. Keeping fabric my foundation, I wandered through the house, looking and thinking. What did I need? What did I want to make? And what was practical for others to make from the delightful stuff that is cloth? Sewing home goods is (thankfully) something we can all do and, as well as being both simple and satisfying, textiles add that ever-important layer of colour, pattern and texture that convert a house into something much more indefinable – our home.

Cloth is, of course, my thing – fabric shops have been my go-to-place for happy browsing since I was a kid. I have spent many years roaming stores and markets looking for the fabric that 'speaks to me' – whether vintage, velvet or floral, you always know when a piece of cloth is perfect for you and your home. Uncut fabric is obviously pure magic, the rows of bolts thrilling and the stroking with a flat palm is, of course, unavoidable. I have always loved the thwack of the bolt of cloth on a cutting bench and the excitement of the purchase – with pattern in hand and deep in covert discussion with the attentive assistant, the promise of textile nirvana just a snip and stitch away.

I am a true advocate of making and there is real joy in making quilts and curtains, cushions and napkins that you need or want for your home. Sometimes we make because we want to learn something new, other times because we can make something better than 'a bought one'. Good quality fabric is worth every penny but you can still usually make something for less outlay than the ready-made alternative. When you make, it is also the opportunity to express yourself, your home and what you love – 'I'm free to be me'.

When I teach, I'm often surprised that, although every participant is eager and able to express their own style through their clothing choices, they can be paralysed when it comes to their home. Of course, a sweater is easier to donate to charity than a sofa and it is harder to visualise a whole room than take stock of an outfit in front of the mirror. But cushions and curtains, napkins and quilts are all easy ways to express your creativity. Sometimes you just have to give in to it.

All of the projects in *Home Sewn* can be altered to fit your aesthetic vibe. The patchwork curtain panels can become a riot of colour, the ottomans a floral bouquet or the pinboard a vintage toile. Take the essence of the project and make it yours. Try not to be swayed by my metallic leather – instead look at the lines or shape of the project, because that's the most important part of any design.

So I needed and wanted everything I've designed and made for *Home Sewn*. After the wandering and thinking about our home, I worked out what I wanted to make and almost every item is resting within. The tablecloth sparkled under our annual Christmas party buffet (a most excellent party) and the quilted throw – well, Lily (pooch number 1) is lying under – yes under – that next to me. The ottomans have held toddlers for naps and teenagers for daydreams, and the chair cover is still holding my fragile pink chair together. I could go on, but needless to say every room in our home is brought to life with these things, each of which tells a little of our story.

Some of the projects are simple to make, but all have a place, either to fulfil practical needs or provide a necessary dose of whimsy. The key is to make – that's all.

living

'God is in the detail' – *or why you need lamps*

antique linen lampshade

Why are lampshades so expensive? Some should be because they are couture-like in their construction. Wonderful pleating and gathering, ribbon trims and bespoke shapes. Others are simply because they just are, it seems.

A simple drum lampshade is constructed in the same manner whether you are using expensive French silk or block print cotton. I think it comes down to the mystery of them – they do look unbelievably difficult to make, but in fact they take about 30–40 minutes, if you go about it in a calm and measured manner. They're not difficult, but you do have to concentrate.

Making lampshades has become even easier in the last few years because you can buy a complete kit of the innards and tools (with instructions) for a very reasonable sum of money. You can now immerse yourself in a new textile craft that is both useful and personal. And let's not forget it's another reason to buy more cloth…

I've made all of the lampshades in our home and regularly switch them with the seasons and/or whim. I've made them from African kuba cloth, hand-dyed silk and many from linen that I pick up from antique fairs. One antique linen sheet will make three to four shades, which is great value, but lampshades also add texture and softness to a room. You can use any fine to medium-weight fabric, but remember that patterned fabric will throw that pattern around the room when the lamp is on and the colour of fabric can vary considerably between the on and off switch.

You can make shades for lamp, wall and ceiling lights, and can make them in many sizes and shapes – just choose the correct kit. You can look at lamps in department and antique stores to see the shapes and proportions that work well together – it isn't an arduous task and you may find a super lamp base…

You'll need:

A lampshade kit from www.needcraft.co.uk. They have created a variety of kits to make the lampshade(s) of your dreams, so find the shape and style to work with your base or room. In your kit will be a set of rings, the sticky, heat-resistant plastic liner, double-sided tape and a plastic tool that looks like a pointy comb, plus the instructions and links to useful videos.

Fabric. How much you'll need depends on the size of the shade you are making. For some perspective, 1m of 140cm-wide linen will easily make three 40cm drum shades.

You'll also need:

Iron with steam option

Fabric scissors

To make:

1 Read the kit instructions to become familiar with the process of making a lampshade. There are also plenty of videos on the supplier's website, which are really helpful to watch.

2 Gather everything together and check the amount of fabric that you'll need. Cut and press your fabric. Making a lampshade is best done standing, so clear a space at a dining or work table.

3 Lay your fabric right side down and lay the plastic liner on top. Cut the excess fabric but leave at least 20mm at the long edges and 15mm at each of the short ends so that you can trim and stick the fabric back for a neat finish.

4 Peel a section of the plastic from the sticky backing. Lay this sticky side down on the fabric, keeping the fabric straight and taut. Continue peeling and sticking until complete. Turn the lampshade fabric side up and smooth out any last wrinkles.

5 Use the double-sided tape provided to stick the fabric on the short edges to the inside of the shade. Trim the fabric on the long edges either to 10mm, or, if your kit has pre-scored lines, trim to the edge of the plastic, then remove the two thin strips of plastic. This will make perfect sense once you have your kit.

6 Use the double-sided tape to coat the pair of rings. It's slightly fiddly, so pause and watch the aforementioned videos as this is where it can go a little wrong …

7 Place the rings, parallel to each other, one on each of the long edges. Roll the rings forward at the same time. Watch that your rings don't slide off the edge as you roll or that you catch the excess fabric.

8 When you get to the end you will have a slight overlap. Place a strip of double-sided tape on the inside of the outer edge to adhere the two short edges together. Press firmly together.

9 To complete your shade, you need to tuck the excess fabric along the top and bottom edges over and behind the ring. Gently does it is my advice. Start by clipping the fabric at the three prongs on the ring with the bulb fitting. Roll the fabric around the ring, then using a pushing motion, tuck it behind the ring with the comb edge of the tool provided. Finally, slide the pointed edge around the inside of the ring. This tidies away the last straggly bits.

10 Repeat this for the open ring. You won't need to clip the fabric first – and then you're done.

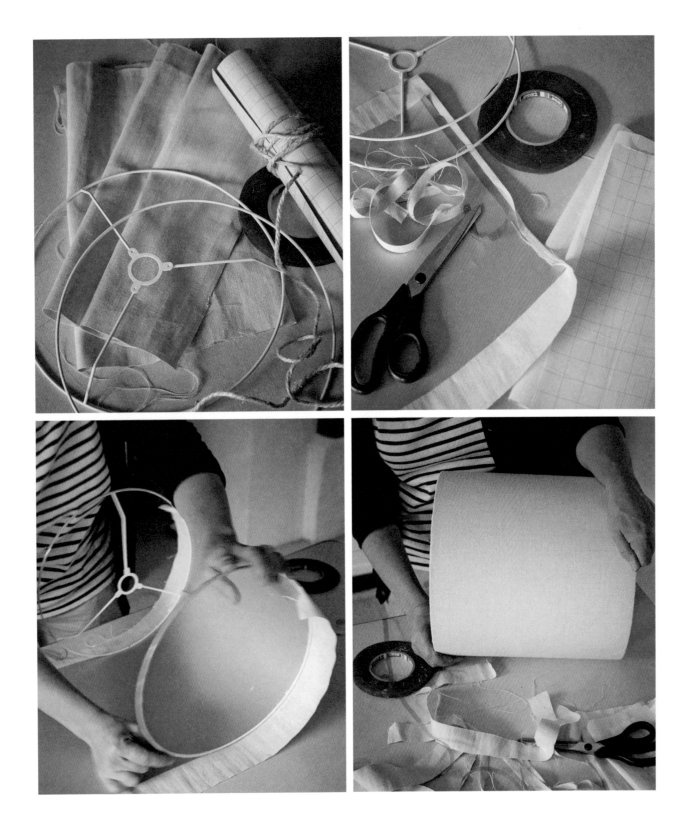

linen ottomans

The eternally useful ottoman

The ottomans win! My absolute favourite project in *Home Sewn*.

They are, of course, completely practical and enormously attractive and, well, quite simply, they're the final piece in the seating puzzle. The footrest, dog nest or toddler sleeping spot, they provide a casual counterpoint to everything else. Of course they're great for languid teenage assemblies and a few shoved together could, at a push, be pressed into service as an extra bed option. How about the just-bought-a-flat-furniture-free conundrum? Needless to say how useful a gift of a couple of ottomans would be there.

For my ottomans, I used the remainder of some antique linen sheets and a piece from a bolt of linen. And, just because I felt like it, I dyed the ivory linen an unplanned shade of pink. I had some ageing blackberries and, rather than bin them, I made a natural dye – with an excellent end result.

I hope you're sold on these as much as I am. A last sales pitch would be to tell you how easy they are to make.

You'll need:

The ottomans are 55 x 17cm square/deep.

1.2m of 140cm wide fabric. It needs to be medium- to heavy-weight, so upholstery, wool or antique linen would do a fine job. If you don't have quite enough fabric, you can cut the base from another fabric, as this won't be seen.

1 x 36cm zip

Matching cotton thread. You can also use contrasting thread for topstitching.

Stuffing of your choice. I used up bags and bags of fabric scraps – it's surprising how much you need and it does make them quite heavy. You can use old clothes, duvets or cushion inners, or even beanbag filler if you would like a lighter option. Up to you really.

You'll also need:

Iron with steam option

Pins and fabric scissors

Pencil (mechanical is best but a freshly sharpened one will do)

Sewing machine with a zipper foot

Paper scissors

Sellotape, sticky tape or paper glue

To make:

1 Go to www.cassandraellis.co.uk/homesewn and download the pdf pattern file marked 'ottoman'. This is delivered as a print-at-home pattern so you'll just need access to an A4 or US letter printer. You'll also need paper scissors and either sellotape, sticky tape or paper glue. All other information is provided on the pdf file.

2 Lay out your fabric and pin the pattern pieces to the fabric, following the correct grainline. Use your pattern pieces to guide you. Cut one top, four sides and two bottoms.

3 Pin the four sides right sides together at the short ends and sew 1cm seams. Press the seams flat then open. If using linen or wool remember to use a pressing cloth (see page 150). Topstitch both sides of each seam.

4 Sew the two bottom pieces right sides together from the edge to where the zip will be inserted. Use the standard foot and a normal length straight stitch. Then baste the remaining seam closed. You can hand baste or use the longest stitch possible on your sewing machine. Press the seam open.

5 Pin the closed zip face down and centred on the basted seam. Change to the zipper foot. Sew the zip into place. Turn over to the right side and topstitch around the ends and two sides of the zip. Unpick the basted seam and press. Unzip the zip so that you can turn the ottoman right side out later.

6 Pin the bottom to the sides, right sides together and lining up the corner notches with the sides seams. Sew a 1cm seam. Press, then clip the seams at the corners. Repeat to attach the top to the sides.

7 Turn right side out and press again. Topstitch around the top and bottom seams to finish the ottoman. One last press and then fill with the stuffing of your choice.

cotton and antique silk
scrappy quilt sofa throw

When scraps become greater than the sum of their parts

Happily, this quilt is a very simple and flexible entrée into the world of quilting. It's about using up your scraps and fabric treasures – and it really is very straightforward to put together. I know many people are a bit overwhelmed at the thought of making a quilt – don't be – at its core a quilt is just fabric cut into bits and then sewn back together. Totally simple. But, of course, it's much more than that. It takes your time and thought and probably uses fabrics that have meaning for you. And when it's completed, it will provide warmth and comfort to someone who is important to you. Remember that making a quilt isn't a competition nor a mathematical test – it's usually an act of love and respect.

This quilt is made up from three different-sized pieces that are joined together to make a larger block. This block is then joined with others to make rows, which come together to form the quilt. When sewn and quilted, you don't see the regimented rows, just the individual pieces of cloth. It's quite special for a scrappy little number.

You'll need:

This quilt is 150 x 150cm, however each block within it is 15 x 30cm, so the design is completely flexible for all bed (or sofa) sizes. The template is created for you to use up all the small pieces and scraps of cloth that you have – perfect for using children's clothes or leftover fabric from other projects. It needs roughly 3.5m of fabric for the front and 3m for the back, but it all depends on the fabric piles you are drawing from.

You'll also need approximately 0.5m of fabric for the binding – again something new or something from fabrics you already have.

180 x 180cm wadding of your choice. You can buy wadding as a precut roll for the quilt size you are making.

Matching cotton thread plus contrasting thread for basting

Cotton quilting thread in the colour of your choice if hand quilting

You'll also need:

Iron with steam option

Sewing machine

Pins and fabric scissors

Basting needle

Quilting needle if hand-quilting

Quilter's ruler and cutting mat (Alternatively, you can use scissors, a long ruler and pencil instead.)

Pencil with soft lead

Tailor's chalk or dressmaker's pencil

Masking tape (if hand quilting)

To make:

1 Wash, dry and press all of your fabric. Sort your fabric into loose piles – anything very small, put to one side and then sort by colour or pattern. Cut your fabric into the three sizes: 7 x 12cm, 12 x 12cm and 12 x 17cm. You will need about four times as many 7 x 12cm pieces as the other two sizes. You don't need to cut all the fabric at once nor do you need to plan the exact number of pieces at the start. My 150 x 150cm throw needed 50 of the 12 x 17cm pieces, 50 of the 12 x 12cm pieces and 200 of the 7 x 12cm pieces, but I cut quite a few more just so that I had a bigger choice of fabrics.

2 Line your cut pieces up into piles, first by size, then by pattern – you need to be able to see them clearly.

3 Your seam allowance is 1cm and is already built into the cut sizes. You should have a 1cm marker on your sewing machine, but if not, then simply draw a line with a soft pencil, or place a small piece of tape at the 1cm mark.

4 Referring to the pattern below, start by sewing pairs of shapes 1 and 2 together (50 pairs in total for this size throw). Just choose two different pieces – you'll find a rhythm will come easily. Sew right sides together. You can sew these as a chain for speed's sake. Press all the seams flat, then open. Sew shapes 3, 4 and 5 together (50 sets again) in the same way. Press the seams flat, then open.

5 Line these two piles up and again choose one of each to sew together, rights sides facing. Press the seam flat, then open.

6 Finally sew each of these sets to a shape 6. Take a little more time with choosing these combinations to make sure the different fabrics are evenly distributed. Press the seams flat, then open and press again.

7 Clear a floor or table space that is larger than the quilt. Lay out the blocks in a combination that you find pleasing. The 150 x 150cm quilt takes five blocks across each of ten rows. Take photos with your phone or ipad to remind you of successful combinations before you commit.

8 Sew the rows together horizontally, short end to short end. I find this prevents the seams twisting. Press all the seams, then pin the first pair of rows together, right sides facing and taking care to line up the seams. Sew, then press. Repeat for the remaining rows. Trim loose threads, press again and your quilt top is complete.

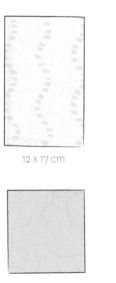

12 x 17 cm

7 x 12 cm

12 x 12 cm

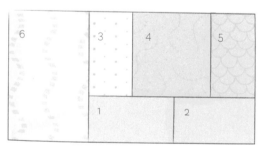

antique linen and silk roll-up blinds

A beautiful blind for a favourite room

My favourite room in our home is what I refer to as the garden room. It isn't in the garden; rather it hovers above it in a Rapunzel-like fashion. But the window was naked and needed something – something that didn't mask the view but provided the option of coverage if needed. Curtains would be too heavy and not often closed. I also wanted to make something simple rather than a full-on complicated roman blind. Unlikely to go up and down on a daily basis, a roll-up blind seemed like the best textile solution from both a construction and visual point of view. This will be a blind of texture, pattern and all-round pleasingness – and quick to make! This is the blind for workrooms and spare rooms, garden sheds and anywhere else that needs an effortless solution.

And so to the cloth. An antique linen sheet – thankfully earmarked for this project whilst there was still enough to make it – with a backing in silk sari. This isn't overly practical as sun and silk is not a good long-term marriage. I have no excuse except that it was embroidered with gold, so impossible not to use it. I made it and it is a visual success. It also makes me exceedingly happy.

You'll need:

Fabric for both the front and back of your blind (see step 1, page 26 for measuring up)

Two wooden battens a few mm shorter than the width of your finished blind. You may need to cut these down with a light hacksaw or have them cut by a local DIY store/lovely neighbour.

Matching cotton thread

A packet of screw eyes and hooks

Cord or thin rope

A cleat (not compulsory but if you have children or naughty puppies, it is best to secure the cords on a cleat, making sure it is out of reach of the small people and pooches)

You'll also need:

Iron with steam option

Pressing cloth

Pins, a hand-sewing needle and fabric scissors

Long ruler or quilter's ruler

Pencil (mechanical is best but a freshly sharpened one will do)

Sewing machine

To make:

Although the instructions below may read as a lengthy process, it really isn't – just many short steps with an excellent end result.

1 Measure the window's width and height. You would usually hang a roll-up blind inside the window frame, so these are the measurements you'll need. Add 2cm to the width and 10cm to the length to create the correct cutting size. Draw these measurements onto the back of each fabric and cut. Then decide which fabric you would like to be the front of the blind.

2 With the two fabrics right sides facing, pin and sew a 1cm seam down each long edge. Press the seams, then turn right side out and press again. Check you are using the correct iron temperature for the fabrics you are using and use a pressing cloth on linen or wool.

3 On the top edge of the blind, fold 2cm to the wrong side. Press, then fold over 3cm and press again. Pin, then sew to form a casing for the batten. Repeat for the bottom of the blind, then insert the battens. Hand-sew the four open ends closed. It's best to do the rest of the making at a table or workbench – wrangling with cords on floors often leads to knotty disasters.

4 Screw two eyelets through the fabric, into the top edge of the top batten approximately 8–12cm in from the edge. Then screw two eyelets directly below these but on the front of the blind.

5 Screw another eyelet into the base of the top batten, 5cm from the edge of the blind. Make sure this is on the side of the window that you want to place the cleat.

6 Cut two lengths of cord/rope, one at three times the length of the blind, the other three-and-a-half times.

7 Tie one end of each piece of cord to an eyelet at the top of the blind, making sure the longer piece is tied to the eyelet on the non-cleat side.

8 Drop the cords down the back of the blind, then bring around the front. Thread them through the eyelets on the front of the top batten, then through the rogue but essential extra eyelet. Knot the lengths of cord together at the ends and trim any excess.

9 Measure and mark the correct placement for the two matching hooks on the window frame, by holding the blind up to the inside of the window. Fix the hooks and lower the top eyelets onto the hooks. You can then raise and lower the blind by pulling the cords.

10 Screw a cleat onto the wall or window frame. Wrap the cord around the cleat to fix it in place or loosely knot the cord if you prefer a more jaunty/dishevelled look.

embroidered lambskin and silk throw pillows

Cushion + leather + metallic thread + wabi sabi style embroidery
= something really very beautiful/modern/handmade

I've just counted the number of cushions in our house. It could possibly be seen as obsessive but I'm not dwelling on that. They are the simplest way to indulge your textile obsession. You can change them on a whim, the seasons or not at all. You can use almost any textile – including leather – and so I thought, why not? I have a thing about metallic leather (again, it's a 'signature' – lawks!). But I have a thing about metallic in general. It's my pattern of choice right down to my shoes. So soft leather with metallic thread is a natural combination. You may have a thing for yellow paired with 1930s bark cloth – give into it!

Cushions are, of course, useful. How else are we meant to make nests for pets or a soft landing for tired heads? Of course, too many is silly – nobody needs eight on a bed. But they are great for extra sofa-squash-and-burrowing options. They are also opportunities for total personalisation and a very simple entry point to sewing for your home. If it's all you ever make, that's enough (do try the ottomans too, please!). A top tip is to try not to make the cushions too full and firm, otherwise they look and feel like cereal boxes in a row. You want a good measure of squish.

The stitching for this cushion is a total homage to Japanese Boro stitching – which I am deeply in love with. It's also very simple – imperfect stitching being perfect. A few crosses, hatches or lines to create something very beautiful. Thus metallic thread hand-stitched through very soft leather to make a cushion that I adore – and a most excellent gift, I might add.

You'll need:

A piece of very fine, soft glove, clothing or lining leather. Choose your finished cushion size and buy a piece at least 3cm larger all round.

A piece of backing fabric the same size. I used a very beautiful piece of Indian block-printed silk. I have used it in the Silk quilt throw on page 21 and it seemed like the perfect contrast to the gold and ivory on the front.

Feather and down cushion inner in the size of your choice

Matching cotton thread

Metallic embroidery thread

You'll also need:

Fabric scissors

Pencil with soft lead

Small bulldog clips

Sewing machine with a walking foot

Embroidery needle

Long metal ruler

To make:

1 Start with your embroidery. Thread your needle with a double thickness of metallic thread, knot and, bringing the needle through from the back, simply stitch crosses, single lines or hatches. I roughly worked out a circular shape slightly off centre for mine, but you can create any format. Continue stitching until you are happy.

2 Lay the leather flat on a table. Measure and draw the size of your cushion plus 3cm all round, then cut out. Trace this shape onto the backing fabric and cut out. Place the two pieces wrong sides facing and use the clips to hold them together.

3 With the walking foot attached, sew around all four sides with a 1cm seam allowance, leaving a large gap to slide the cushion inner through. Carefully put the inner inside the cover. Then machine stitch the opening closed.

4 With sharp scissors, carefully trim the raw edges down to approximately 5mm.

gilded silk organdie butterflies

Why whimsy is wonderful

Fabric is definitely in our nests to fulfil function, but I also encourage you to use it to make something beautiful — for beauty's sake alone. As much as quilts and cushions are opportunities for personal expression, often it's the naïve and uncomplicated things we create that colour in our story. And a little bit of gratuitous ephemera in our homes is always good.

So, to butterflies — a fleeting but uplifting sight and ongoing proof that beauty can come from anywhere. Although I don't envy their lifespan, I do envy their freedom and flight. A visual reminder of childhood, love, liberty and the passing of time.

I'm not quite sure where this project idea came from but I have a note saying 'wall of butterflies — how lovely' in my sketchbook. Whilst strolling through town I popped into my favourite art store — there were rows of bottles of liquid gilt, every colour, every nuance. I love the art of gilding — who wouldn't want to work with leaves of gold and silver? Finally, fossicking through my favourite fabric street unearthed a scrap of silk organdie — and there it was.

Today a flurry of gilded butterflies climbs my studio walls, catching the light and preparing for flight. I can't begin to tell you the pleasure it brings me and all who visit.

You'll need:

0.25–0.5m of stiff silk organza or cotton organdie

1 or 2 pots of liquid gilt. Choose your own colours. You can use metallic paint or fabric paint if you prefer.

Fine metal pins or entomology pins

Pincushion

Artist's paintbrushes. These don't have to be great quality, but you will need several and one with a very fine tip.

You'll also need:

Small thread scissors

Pencil (mechanical is best, but freshly sharpened will do)

Decorator's plastic dustsheet

Decorator's gloves

Paint cleaner

To make:

1 This is a lovely way to while away an hour or so. Start by tracing out your butterfly shapes. Go to www.cassandraellis.co.uk/homesewn and download the pdf pattern files marked Butterflies. This is a print at home A4/US letter pattern sheet. As the organdie is transparent, you can just move the fabric over the butterfly and, using a pencil, trace as many butterflies as you would like. Then cut out, cutting just inside your pencil lines if you can.

2 Lay the dustsheet on a table. Wearing gloves, paint each butterfly with the colour or colours of your choice.

3 Whilst they are drying, you can then carefully paint the heads of the pins with a contrasting colour. Use a tiny brush and have a pincushion to hand to stick the pins in to dry.

4 Once the butterflies are dry, crease them through the centre so that they become three-dimensional.

5 Carefully place a pin through the centre of a butterfly and push it gently, on an angle, into a wall, ceiling or pinboard of your choice. You will create tiny pinprick holes, so make sure you are happy with this and that they are in a safe position for your home and it's inhabitants.

Wonderful whimsy indeed.

A modern take on a patchwork cushion

leather and linen patchwork cushions

I bet you made (or attempted to make) a patchwork cushion in sewing class at school. It was on the list alongside the A-line skirt and pencil case. All ugly. I don't know about you, but I have never attempted any of these things again. The unpleasant combination of a teacher barking out 'unpick your seams' and the a—ppall—ing fabric options was surely enough to halt all but the most ardent of sewers.

To revisit that patchwork cushion is, I realise, a bold move. It could quickly fall into the pits of plain rather than simple yet chic, but I'm giving it a go. To really push the boat out, I'm giving you three different design options. I also realise that I may love leather as a home textile more than some. You can, of course, use any fabric you want for these cushions — felted wool would be gorgeous, as would velvets, silks or vintage scraps.

You'll need:

Leather or suede scraps. Use as fine a weight as possible – it's usually called glove, clothing or lining leather.

Linen for the 'frame' on the front and as backing for the cushion cover. You'll need 0.25–0.5m, depending on the size and design.

1 x zip (if you want a zippered closure)

Matching cotton thread

1 x feather and down cushion inner

DESIGN 1 The cushion cover front is all leather and the finished size is 30 x 40cm. You will need approximately 2 square feet of leather (it's always measured in feet), although leather is sold as a complete hide or piece of a hide. You will also need a piece of linen at least 42 x 40cm. Decide if you are finishing the cushion with either a zip or a simple slipstitch closure to work out the exact quantity. You will also need a feather and down cushion inner of 30 x 40cm.

DESIGN 2 This is the long, lean framed design with a finished size of 30 x 60cm. You will need just under 1 square foot of leather and approximately 0.4m of linen for the front and back. Make the same finishing choices as for Design 1. You will also need a 30 x 60cm feather and down cushion inner.

DESIGN 3 This simple framed square uses the least leather of all, so if you just have a few scraps this would be ideal. Less than 1 square foot of leather is needed. The cushion has a finished size of 45 x 45cm and needs just under 0.5m of linen to finish, plus a 45cm cushion inner. Choose your closure option.

You'll also need:

Fabric scissors

Pencil (mechanical is best but a freshly sharpened one will do)

Ruler. A quilter's ruler would be the easiest option to create perfect squares and triangles.

Sewing machine with a needle for sewing leather, and a walking foot.

Iron with a steam option.

To make:

1 Cut out your leather. For Design 1, measure and cut 20 x 12cm squares. For Design 2, you'll need 5 x 12cm squares and Design 3 needs 4 x 12cm squares. Then cut the squares in half to create triangles.

2 Make sure your sewing machine needle is changed to a leather needle (these are easy to buy from haberdashery stores) and if you have a walking foot, pop this on now. Set the machine to a longer length stitch – around 3.5. Spread your triangles out so that you can choose pairs that work together. With right sides facing, sew pairs of triangles back together, along the diagonal edge, using a 1cm seam. Finger press the seams flat and snip away the 'ears'. Continue sewing pairs together until you have 20, 5 or 4 squares depending on the design you are making.

3 FOR DESIGN 1, sew four rows of five squares together using 1cm seams. Finger press the seams and snip away the 'ears' and loose thread. Then sew the four rows together, carefully lining up the seams. Finger press and snip – the cushion front is complete.

FOR DESIGN 2, sew one row of five squares together with 1cm seams. Finger press the seams and snip away the 'ears' and loose threads. Cut two pieces of linen 42 x 13cm and two pieces 12 x 32cm. With right sides facing

and the leather on top, sew the patchwork to one of the longer pieces of linen on the long edge with a 1cm seam. Repeat for the other long edge. Carefully press the seam on the linen only. Repeat this for the two short edges so that you have created a frame. Carefully press and the cushion front is complete.

FOR DESIGN 3, sew two rows of two squares together using 1cm seams. Finger press and snip away the 'ears' and loose threads. Join these two rows to form a square, then finger press and snip. Cut two pieces of linen 16.5 x 16.5cm and two pieces 16.5 x 47cm. Create a frame as for Design 2, except sewing the short pieces first. Carefully press.

4 If you want a simple slipstitch closure, then cut a piece of linen the same size as the front. Sew the two pieces together with a 1cm seam, right sides facing. Leave a gap to insert the cushion, press, clip the corners and turn right side out. Slide the cushion inner inside and carefully slipstitch closed.

5 If you would like to create a zip finish, then cut a piece of linen the same length as the cushion front, but 2cm wider. Fold, press and cut in half. Follow the instructions from the Antique silk scrap bed bolsters on pages 90–93 to insert the zip and finish the cushion.

block-printed cotton
Boro throw

Why patching is good for the soul

My love for Boro runs deep. Boro is beautiful – aesthetically, of course, but its true beauty lies in the spirit and the hands of the makers creating it. You see Boro is made from rags. The Japanese had an idea called mottainai – that scraps of cloth were too good to waste. So these almost useless remnants were stitched to other scraps to create something extremely useful, but also very, very beautiful. Even more so than quilts, Boro are the ultimate storyteller of family. These blankets and throws were continually added to and then passed down generation after generation. Lives began and concluded in the folds of the fabric. As you stitch over an ancestor's stitch, you are connected.

My Boro blanket was the very last project I made for this book. I also spent far too much time choosing fabric – a tightly edited selection of basic but beautiful cloths and then the special ones on top. It took many, many trips to my favourite stores to find the silks, block prints and khadi cottons – the fabric loves of my life, really. I also kept the scraps from all the other projects because I knew I would make (the beginnings of) a Boro blanket.

This is the simplest kind of sewing – hand-stitching cloth to cloth. Mending tears and holes with whatever is to hand. I'd like to think this is something you won't ever finish, nor your children, nor theirs. Shall we begin your family Boro?

You'll need:

Fabric. You will need one piece of cloth for the front and one piece for the back as a base for your Boro blanket. This can be any size and you can join fabrics together if you want to. Make your choices on what you have available and what you'd like to be at the base of your stitching journey. I have had a piece of old Indian block print for some years. It has obviously been used and washed many times, so although the fabric is beautifully soft, it was also a little worn. Top result, I thought, as here was the perfect base. The blanket is simply the size of this piece of fabric once it was trimmed and straightened – about 1.2 x 1.5m. I then used the last antique linen sheet as its backing.

You'll also need a pile of fabric scraps – again, no preset size or number.

Matching cotton thread and contrasting thread for the Boro patches

You'll also need:

Iron with steam option

Pins and fabric scissors

Sewing machine

Hand-sewing needles

To make:

1 Wash, dry and press all the fabrics. Decide on the base size of your Boro blanket. Cut (and piece if necessary) a top and bottom to the same size. Pin these together, right sides facing. Sew all the way around with a 1cm seam allowance, leaving a 15cm opening. Press the seams and clip the corners. Turn the blanket right side out and press again. Slipstitch the opening closed.

2 All you need to do now is cut and stitch scraps to your base cloth. You can apply just to the top or top and bottom. Obviously start by repairing any tears or holes to make the blanket robust, but the rest is up to you. You can hand-stitch using a simple Kantha/running stitch or use the Boro stitch technique I used for the embroidered leather pillow (see pages 29–30). Obviously, choice of thread and colour is totally yours too.

decorative silk
upholstery panels

Small fragments can create great beauty

As well as my much-mentioned hoard of practical cloth, I have an equally large collection of decorative textile fragments. Morsels of antique embroidery and snippets of silk all sitting and waiting… Many come together in a quilt but others are just there for inspiration. In one special box are my scraps of hand-dyed silk velvet. I love it, but it's awkward stuff – a veritable nightmare to sew, so when it gets to scraps, I cannot build sufficient interest into sewing it to something else. I could, of course, frame my most favourite pieces – this looks fantastic and can be a great visual reminder of something important to you (like framing baby's first shoes – cute!). But I thought of something else – what about a little primitive upholstery action on one of the many chairs in our house. This creates the same effect as framing but with added tactility. It can sit there looking beautiful until I either tire of it or want to try something new, or get my act together and get the chairs properly upholstered – a day that may never come.

Ridiculously simple – and like the butterfly wall and the fabric chandelier, aesthetically positively indispensible.

You'll need:

A chair with an upholstered back. Don't use anything very expensive – something 'in need of work' will thank you most for this approach.

A piece of fabric larger than the chair back.

You'll also need:

Upholstery tacks

Small hammer

Fabric scissors

Small thread scissors

To make:

You probably don't need instructions – the images say almost all you need. But here we go:

1 Lay the chair down on its back. Lay the piece of fabric over the area you want to 'upholster' and roughly cut a shape a little larger. Start at the centre top of the chair and lightly hammer the tacks through the fabric. Then move to the centre bottom and place a few more tacks. Keep the fabric taut as you work your way across to complete the top and bottom. Repeat this step for the centre sides. Then pull the fabric firmly and finish tacking the sides, remembering to tuck and fold into the corners. Trim the excess if you require and then admire/ be inspired.

You can, of course, paint or gild some cloth, embroider it, give some fabric to your children to paint or draw on – anything that takes your fancy really.

leather beanbag bookends

How to corral your piles of paper – or books

I left the windows open in the studio unattended. I came back to find paper patterns scattered everywhere, including out of said windows – utter disaster. I could/should have used one of my many stones to hold the piles in their correct order, but I didn't – partly because they were too small but mostly because I didn't want to mess with my carefully arranged stone vignettes – good grief! Creative work is all the better for a little organisation – a little pile shuffling and corralling is necessary for a clear head – because if everything is everywhere, then it's difficult to get on with the job of being creative isn't it? Of course this applies to organising your bills too…

And then I had a wheeze. I'll make something – something heavy-ish but something nice to hold. It's not a big leap to go from the idea of a doorstop to a paperweight, but leap I did. And then I thought, if I get it right, they'll be pretty bang perfect as bookends too. And so, some size experimentation and weighty content options looked into, and I've made something that works a treat. As a bonus, the leather makes them very tactile and for an inanimate object, very cute. Cute wasn't planned at all, but they look like a pudgy non-toy toy. Weird but they work.

You'll need:

Leather. A piece 30 x 40cm and up to 1.2mm thick will make one bookend/paperweight.

Dry rice

Matching cotton thread

You'll also need:

Fabric scissors

Pencil (mechanical is best but a freshly sharpened one will do)

Ruler

Sewing machine with a needle for sewing leather

Kitchen funnel

Darning needle

To make:

1 It's a 20-minute job – tops. Cut two pieces of leather 17 x 27cm. With right sides facing, sew a 1cm seam all around, leaving a 5–7cm gap. Trim the corners, finger press the seams and turn right side out, gently poking the corners out.

2 Use the kitchen funnel as a conduit to fill the leather bag with rice. Be careful not to overfill, as you want them to have some flexibility/personality.

3 If your sewing machine can take it, sew the opening closed. If not, carefully hand-stitch it closed. This isn't the easiest task, but relatively quick.

One weirdly cute but extremely useful paperweight/bookend/stress reliever completed.

leather strapping curtain tiebacks

If you have curtains that need tying back...

Many of us may not need or want curtain tiebacks anymore, but for those that do, the shop-bought options can be a little limited in choice and expensive for the simple function they perform. If you do need them, you just need something really simple – tactile and good-looking obviously, but simple. The point is to let the light in and to keep your curtains rounded up when necessary. No wrestling with your drapes of a morning, thank you!

My idea is embarrassingly simple – it came from a belt, because I once used a belt to tie back a curtain. Again, not a huge leap from belt to this, but it works and it is a little fantastic, isn't it? I used a 2cm natural leather strap with chrome fittings, but you could go many ways. Glossy black with old brass perhaps or waxed chocolate with nickel. And, as well as a tieback, they can be used as a tie-up for casual blinds. All you need to do is set around ten minutes aside.

You'll need:

Leather straps come in approximately 110cm lengths. It's not exactly precise because leather is obviously not square to start with. They also come in different widths – 15–50mm – and in quite a few colours, thicknesses and finishes. Depending on what you will be tying back, a long thin strap may work better than a short wide strap, or vice versa. The thinner the width, the easier it will be to wrap but the less control over heavy curtains. The choice is yours – and to help, a good supplier is provided at the back of the book on page 154.

One button and washer screw fitting per tieback. These come in a kit with everything you need.

You'll also need:

Fabric scissors

Scalpel

Awl or leather hole punch

Ballpoint pen or pencil with soft lead

To make:

1 Wrap the strap around your curtains to decide how long/how many wraps you'd like. Mark this with pen or pencil, then cut the strap using very sharp scissors or a scalpel. Use a magazine or cutting board underneath as protection.

2 Mark a dot at one end of the strap, centred and at least 2cm in from the end. Lay the strap flat on the board/magazine and make a hole using the awl or leather punch. If using an awl, you may need to wiggle it about to create a hole large enough.

3 Fit the button and washer according to the instructions provided.

4 Mark a 1cm vertical line, at least 2cm in from the remaining end. Create a buttonhole by carefully slicing along this line with the scalpel. Check that the button fits snugly and you're done.

5 When your curtains are drawn, the tiebacks curl up neatly and look rather beautiful.

canvas and rope
log carriers

Bringing the outside in

My husband loves, loves, loves a fire. He loves planning for one, gathering for one and then the final act of making one. But then who doesn't love an open fire? If you live in a city, you probably have to make do with smokeless fuel (for good reason), but if you're lucky enough to be living it large in the countryside, well then, there isn't anything better than a roaring log fire.

In order for him to gather logs when in the country, I thought I'd rustle him up something to bring back his haul. You could load up a bag, fill your arms or find a sturdy bucket (all methods tested – none brilliant), but a purpose-made log carrier is simpler to load and carry, plus it holds more wood, so it seemed a very sensible solution. After some research, I came across a suede log carrier from the 1930s that I thought could easily be updated using the wonder cloth that is waxed canvas. It is marvellous stuff, although you need to make sure you are buying authentic sturdy cloth. Like all fabrics that become on-trend, the market can become flooded with cloth that isn't made well and/or doesn't do its job. Proper waxed canvas is expensive, thus no stockpile of it for me...

Handsome it is – and, yes, it works beautifully.

You'll need:

Heavy-weight waxed canvas. Go for as heavy a weight as possible, but make sure you can still sew two layers through your sewing machine. You'll need a piece 50 x 170cm.

1m of 15–20mm wooden dowel (easy to buy from a DIY store)

1.5m of 10mm rope or 3m of thinner rope that you can twist together

Heavy-duty 10mm eyelet kit

Matching cotton thread

You'll also need:

Pins and fabric scissors

Long ruler or quilter's ruler

Tailor's chalk or dressmaker's pencil

Sewing machine

A small saw, or get the DIY store to cut the dowel for you (Don't be tempted to use your bread knife!)

Small hammer

NOTE: you cannot use an iron on waxed canvas, so get your fingers ready for some sturdy finger pressing if you want a crisp fold.

To make:

1 Measure and cut the piece of waxed canvas. Make sure your cuts are clean and straight, as you will not be hemming the sides.

2 Fold over one short end by 15cm and pin – either side is fine, as waxed canvas does not have a right or wrong side. Mark a line 2cm from the folded edge and sew two parallel rows of stitching. This creates the pocket for the dowling. Test the dowling in the pocket – it needs to be a snug fit. If it isn't, take it out and add another row of stitching. Sew the raw folded edge down with two further rows of parallel stitching. Repeat for the second short end.

3 Measure and mark four points for the eyelet holes – 10cm across and down is approximately the right spot. If you mark one in position, you can then copy or line up the remaining ones from that. I suggest you practise inserting one eyelet on a spare piece of cloth, because once the hole is made – its made! Slide a chopping board or old magazine underneath to avoid any furniture damage (voice of experience). Insert your eyelets as per the instructions on the packet, centring the eyelet hole on your pencil mark.

A word of warning. Eyelets are unerringly addictive, as you can add them to all sorts of household goods to make said goods more useful. Turn a tea towel into an apron with two eyelets and two pieces of cotton tape. Done that – excellent result. Sew up a batch of simple flat cotton bags and then bang an eyelet into the corner – et voila – hanging storage. I'll stop here, but I'm sure you get the idea.

4 Cut your rope in two. If you are using the thinner rope, fold the length in half and twist the two strands together (look at mine). Put each end through the eyelets on one side, with the ends on the inside. Knot each end firmly. Repeat with the second piece of rope on the other end of the carrier. Slide the dowling into each pocket and you're done.

A beautiful harbour

patchwork organdie
room dividers

I really love these panels. They sum up our home – and what I love about the idea of home – perfectly. Crafted, emotive, tactile and functional, but also very simple. I based the design and philosophy of these panels on the Korean Pojagi cloth. Pojagi were made to be useful. They carried or wrapped everything from food to gifts, but they also carried great symbolic meaning. Love, respect and happiness for the recipient were all wrapped inside. So I thought how lovely it would be to sleep inside their translucent protection. I hope my very humble homage keeps the two of us safe and happy.

Of course, you could make these for your children as something for them to daydream behind (how wonderful), or as a curtain for a special room. Really they could and should be made for anywhere or anyone you want to 'wrap', if that makes sense.

You'll need:

Cotton organdie or silk organza, which is usually woven in narrow widths of 90–110cm. The fabric needs to feel slightly stiff and be translucent. You can make the panels in any size. To calculate the correct amount of fabric, first measure the space they will hang from, then multiply the height by the width and add 25 per cent as a minimum. Each of my panels is 90 x 220cm and I needed around 5m of fabric to make a pair.

Matching cotton thread

You'll also need:

Iron with steam option

Pins and fabric scissors

Quilter's ruler or set square

Tailor's chalk or dressmaker's pencil

Sewing machine

Cut sizes:

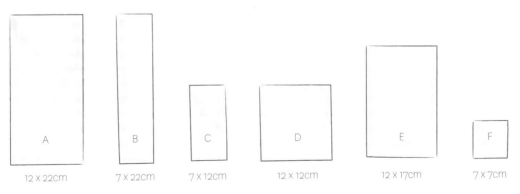

A	B	C	D	E	F
12 x 22cm	7 x 22cm	7 x 12cm	12 x 12cm	12 x 17cm	7 x 7cm

To make:

1 For once, don't wash your fabric – it needs to retain its slightly stiff feel.

2 Set aside roughly one third of your fabric. Measure, mark and cut the remaining fabric into a selection of the sizes shown on the pattern on page 61. As a rough guideline, cut twice as many of the small sizes as the large. Until you start sewing the shapes together, you won't know the exact number you'll require of each. Once you've sewn a good number of blocks together, you'll be able to work out how you should cut the remaining fabric. It does take a little longer to put together, but it will prevent wasting fabric – or worse – running out of options.

3 Look at the different combinations of pieces to make blocks below. Sew pieces of fabric together, using a 1cm seam and the same construction technique as for the sofa throw on pages 21–22. Press the seams flat, then trim them down to 5mm. Your edges will be unfinished.

4 Once you have a number of small blocks, start sewing these together to create larger blocks, pressing and trimming as you go. When you have 8–10 blocks, lay them out on a floor or table and plan how you will fit them together. You might need to add a single piece to another block or rotate a few pieces to make it work. Making one of these panels is like a jigsaw puzzle, but thankfully with more than one solution.

5 Build your first big section to the correct width for a panel, press and set aside. You can then use this as a guide as you continue making.

6 Keep cutting, sewing and jigsaw building until you have a panel the required size.

7 These beautiful panels do take time to make. I admit I was pleased when I snipped the last thread – but I'm even happier with the finished result. To hang, simply use curtain rings and clip hooks.

Block options

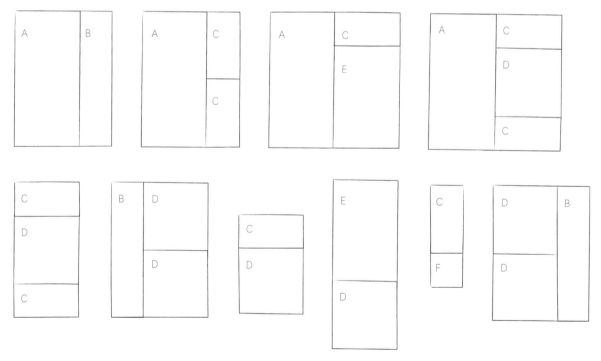

antique linen pendant shade

The pendant shade conundrum

Somewhere in most houses there is a pendant cord hanging from the ceiling and this light fitting is meant to perform luminous miracles. Often hanging in the wrong spot, it casts a nice big shadow instead of the rapturous pools of light you had in mind. A good solution is to reframe the purpose of this light. Make it secondary rather than the main source of light in the room and make something beautiful to hang from it – draw attention to its flaws (imperfect being perfect et al). In this case, the cord-in-the-wrong-spot is saved by a rustic linen lampshade – hand-stitched, rumpled and rather gorgeous. Perfect for spare rooms, odd hallways, student digs or first homes where the budget has been spent on the house itself.

Natural ivory linen casts a lovely light and the construction method means it is totally adaptable for the size of room and height of ceiling. You can use a sewing machine or hand-sew the whole thing if that's your only option. Whatever the shape, fabric or sewing method, this shade is extremely simple to make and costs around the same as the omnipresent cheap paper lantern.

Sometimes, a handmade fabric pendant will actually be exactly what you need, not only for now but also for the foreseeable future.

You'll need:

A 30–35cm-lampshade ring, which attaches to the light fitting. You can buy a complete set, then use the open ring for the chandelier - wheeeeee! - (see page 105), or pull apart an old lampshade.

A strip of wide width linen, at least 120cm wide and a minimum of 50cm long. The linen can be any weight; it depends on the look you want. It's best to choose a pale-coloured linen, as anything dark or patterned will reduce the amount of light available. I used a piece of ivory linen from the bolt I purchased.

Matching cotton thread and contrasting/metallic thread

Rope or cord – optional

You'll also need:

Iron with a steam option

Pins and fabric scissors

Hand-sewing needle

Long ruler or quilter's ruler

Pencil (mechanical is best but a freshly sharpened one will do)

Sewing machine

To make:

1 Cut out a piece of linen 120cm wide by the desired length. Wash the fabric, dry but don't press. You can also scrunch it later if you would like a more rustic look. Fold over 1cm on the two length edges and press carefully. Fold over a further 1cm, then pin. Using your sewing machine, sew these seams down, close to the fold line.

2 Lay the fabric flat and place the ring at the edge of a length edge and 1–2cm in from a long edge. Fold the raw edge over the ring to the wrong side and pin. Roll the ring along and keep pinning until you reach the remaining length edge. You should have a little overlap. Remove the first pin and then re-pin with the overlap.

3 Thread the needle with the contrasting/metallic thread and stitch the layers together around the top edge to secure the ring inside. I used a simple Kantha/running stitch, but you can use any stitch you like. For an extra flourish, hand-stitch down the two length edges.

4 Hang the pendant as a normal pendant light. If the fabric is weighty enough, you could loosely tie it at the bottom. If you do this, make sure you use a very low wattage light bulb and be mindful of inquisitive children's eager hands.

silk velvet and antique sari quilt

And so to bed

This collection of cloth takes me back to where I started with homeware goods, and my zeal for home. When I started designing textiles, I knew I wanted quilts to be part of my story because of what they could mean to someone's home. Quilts are incredibly useful, very personal and therefore beautiful to the maker and recipient. After 15 years of making, I still very much enjoy quilt commissions but I also encourage people to make their own – to tell their story through their hands and choices of cloth. I don't see quilt making as a trend or as a craft to be mastered and displayed. Instead I think it is a very simple way to stitch your family history into something that is to be used and loved. Story-telling at its most practical.

My first quilts (and still my favourite) were seemingly random pieces of fabric, positioned into a pleasing formation. Enthused by the Indian Kantha quilts, I got my 'maths-head' on and drew up my first outwardly 'freestyle' quilt. I dyed silk velvet and hunted down fragments of Japanese kimono and naïve cotton prints. Hooked!

This quilt is the first thing I designed and made for *Home Sewn* – mostly to get myself in the swing of things, but also because the hand-stitching was a committed pasttime over the (many) summer evenings...

Using my hand-dyed velvet, my silks and my Indian block prints, this quilt is reminiscent of where I started and where I'll always come back to.

remove this block for single size quilt

A4   52cm x 12 cm

A3   52 x 57 cm

B1
22 x 82 cm

C1   62 x 22 cm

C3
17 x
172 cm

D4
22 x 67 cm

D5
47 x 67 cm

C2   62 x 152 cm

A1
12 x
102 cm

A2   42 x 102 cm

D6
67 x 72 cm

B2
22 x 52 cm

B3
22 x 82 cm

A5   52 x 47 cm

D1
12 x
37 cm

D2
47 x 37 cm

D3
12 x
37 cm

E4
37 x 42 cm

E3
77 x 42 cm

E2
32 x 32 cm

E1 32 x 12 cm

add a second block for a King/
Super King sized quilt

scale 1:10   seam allowance 1 cm   finished size 210 x 210cm   measurements listed are cutting sizes

You'll need:

The quilt is 210 x 210cm, which is the perfect size for a double or queen-sized bed. If you have a king or super king, then you can make the quilt wider by adding a second column A on the other edge of the quilt (see the pattern opposite). I've marked the pattern so this makes sense. If you are making this for a single bed or as a throw, then remove column A altogether.

You'll need 5–7m of fabric for the front and 5–6m for the back of the quilt. Look at the pattern before you buy/choose your selection of fabrics, as you need to make sure that you have large enough pieces of cloth for the individual sections. You can, of course, just join some further pieces together, so don't worry if you've gone one cut too far...

Use the pattern to plan your placement of cloth. You'll find there is a natural balance between the colours and patterns that you use. You can quickly trace the pattern and colour it in, if you find that helps. Alternatively, you could take the 'go-with-the-flow' approach. Either method is completely correct!

You can use different fabric for your backing or use leftovers from the front. Cotton sheets – old or new – are an excellent idea for the backing too.

You'll also need approximately ½m of fabric for the binding – again something new or something from the remnants from the front or back.

230 x 230cm of wadding of your choice. You can buy wadding as a precut roll for the quilt's size you are making. Remember to increase or reduce this if you are making a different sized quilt.

Matching cotton thread plus contrasting thread for basting

Cotton quilting thread in the colour of your choice (I usually go neutral)

You'll also need:

Iron with steam option

Sewing machine

Pins and fabric scissors

Basting needle

Quilter's ruler and cutting mat. If this is the only time you'd use these, then you can use scissors, a long ruler and pencil instead.

Pencil with soft lead

Tailor's chalk or dressmaker's pencil

Masking tape

To make:

1 Your seam allowance is 1cm and has been built in to your cutting sizes i.e. a 12 x 12cm becomes 10 x 10cm once sewn.

2 Wash, dry and press all of your fabric. Then cut out all your pieces in order, A1–E4, following the measurements on the pattern. You may want to clear a floor space to place your fabrics as you cut them, which will also allow you to adjust your design. Even though I plan everything first, I still do this to give me a little more 'creative license'. As you cut, mark the number of each piece i.e. A1 on the back of the fabric using the soft pencil.

3 This is a very simple quilt to sew together as it has been divided into five blocks, each containing smaller pieces. Start with block A and pin piece A1 to A2, right sides together. Sew then press the seams flat, then open. Pin A3 to A4 right sides together, then sew and press. Pin this block to A1/A2, sew and press. Then repeat to attach A5. Press the whole block.

4 Repeat this process with the remaining four blocks, B–E, simply following the pattern. Press every seam as you go as it ensures a smarter finish.

5 Then join the blocks together in the following order, pressing as you go:

A + B

C + D

C/D + E

A/B + C/D/E.

6 Press again and your quilt top is complete.

7 Your quilt backing needs to be a minimum of 230 x 230cm. Join together your choice of fabric until you have a backing the right size. Press the seams flat, then open. Then press the whole backing again. If you are making a single quilt, your backing needs to be 180 x ⟩⟩⟩

230cm. If King/ Super King it needs to be 280 x 230cm.

8 At this stage, you can send the quilt top, backing and wadding away to a long-arm quilter for quilting and binding (listed in the resource section on page 153). If you want to hand-stitch your quilt, keep reading.

9 If your wadding has been folded, open it out flat and leave it for a few hours to relax the wrinkles.

10 Lay the backing right side down on a clean hard floor space that is larger than the quilt. If you have made your quilt backing out of a mixture of fabric, decide if there is a natural head and foot to it (i.e. the direction it will be on the bed) and plan for this when putting your quilt together.

11 Smooth the backing flat and use masking tape to secure the sides (not the corners as this can distort the backing) to the surface and keep it taut. Lay the wadding on top, making sure it is smooth and matches the backing edges. If the wadding is larger, then trim it down to match the backing.

12 Press your quilt top again and remove any loose threads. Lay the quilt top down right side up on the wadding, making sure it is centred and square to the backing and wadding.

13 Although you can pin your quilt together, I think the simplest method is to baste it with a darning needle and contrasting thread. Working from the top down, baste the layers together using approximately 5cm stitches. You need to create a grid by basting both horizontally and vertically, each row being approximately 10cm apart.

14 Now you can hand-stitch your quilt. Use masking tape and a ruler to create lines to follow or simply free style your stitching as I have done. Use a simple running stitch and don't be tempted to make your thread too long as it will tangle. On a practical level, you need to stitch enough so that the quilt layers are firmly stitched together and won't move about. From an aesthetic point of view, you can stitch as much and in whatever style you please. Remove the basting stitches after you have finished quilting.

15 On to binding. Again you can send this to a long-arm quilter, but if you want to tackle it, read on. You can also look at videos on YouTube for a visual lesson (highly recommended for beginners).

16 Trim the edges of your quilt so that you have four straight sides. Use a long metal ruler and pencil to give you a good guide – pencil in all four lines before you snip, so that you don't over-trim.

17 Measure all four sides of your quilt and add 20cm to calculate the length of binding required. Cut 5cm strips of fabric across the grain. Sew all the strips together into a continuous length and then press the strip in half along the length, wrong sides together.

18 Leave approximately 10cm of the binding strip free. Start at the centre of one side and pin one raw edge of the binding to the edge of the quilt top, right sides together and through all layers. The folded edge of the binding strip will be facing towards the centre of the quilt.

19 Pin the binding all the way around the quilt. When you reach a corner, fold the binding strip to one side and then back on top of itself to make a triangle.

20 Machine sew the binding around the quilt using a 1cm seam allowance. Stop about 0.5cm from the edge of the corner and then start the next seam 0.5cm after the corner.

21 When you get back to the beginning, backstitch and remove the quilt from the sewing machine. Trim off the excess binding and fold and pin the binding under itself. Hand-sew the last few stitches.

22 Fold the binding over to the backside of the quilt and pin. Slipstitch the binding closed all around the quilt.

Good night… and thank you.

How (and why) you should add a little personality to your bedroom

cotton block-printed pillowcases

I have too many pillowcases. Actually, I realised I had too many white pillowcases. Oh yes, some have embroidery and others delightful ladder stitching but they are all varying shades of white and I was getting a little bored... Then I realised that a soupçon of colour and pattern could elevate the bed to another level. It's not about being overly coordinated, just a way of adding your personality into a room that can easily be left a little plain or hotel-like in feel. We spend eight (ok, six and a half for some of us) hours in there a day, so a handmade selection of cushions, quilts and pillowcases can really bring it to (your) life. Time to start dabbling, breaking my all-white mantra.

Bed linen shops are the places of dreams. Who hasn't walked around one with hands held flat in the stroking position? And so on to my quest for a little more personality, I bought some pale rose linen from a favourite store and then... I made a whole lot more, because once you're on a roll, you're on a roll, aren't you? You just need some good-quality cotton or linen cloth. Go ethnic, go vintage, make quirky stuff for your kids' bedrooms. Quilting cotton is perfect for children, both from a print and quality perspective and it isn't expensive. Vintage linen sheets will be a dream and anything floral, striped or hand-printed can add a huge amount of spirit.

I am deeply in love with Indian block-print cotton fabrics – the good ones. The ones you know have been carefully printed by someone who cares and who has been paid properly for their craftsmanship. Oddly, it's quite hard to find a pillowcase made of such – and so I made them. Here's how.

You'll need:

2m of cotton fabric will make a pair of pillowcases with enough to spare for a cushion front or two. The instructions are for standard housewife pillowcases, which measure 50 x 75cm. You can adjust this for European or other sized pillows.

Matching cotton thread

You'll also need:

Iron with steam option

Pins and fabric scissors

Long ruler or quilter's ruler

Tailor's chalk or dressmaker's pencil

Sewing machine

To make:

1 Wash your fabric. If it is hand-dyed, or hand-printed, make sure that the water is running clear as they may not have used a fixative, or they may be a natural dye. If there is still dye-run, boil it in water with some salt added and wash again until the water is crystal clear. Dye-run in your bed would be disastrous so be meticulous with this step. Dry, then press the fabric.

2 To make a pair of pillowcases, measure and cut two pieces of fabric 52 x 78cm and two pieces 52 x 94cm.

3 On one short edge of all four pieces of fabric, fold over and press 1cm towards the wrong side of the fabric. Fold over and press another 1cm. Pin and topstitch just within 1cm. Finish the three remaining edges with an overlocker or zigzag stitch. As you will be washing these pillowcases regularly it's important they have a good finish.

4 To create the envelope closure, lay the first long piece down, right side up with the topstitched edge on the left-hand side. Lay a short piece on top of this, right side down, lining up the raw edges. Make sure the topstitched edge on the short piece is also on the left-hand side.

5 Fold the excess of the long piece over the top of the short piece so that the hemmed edge of the shorter piece meets the fold line. Pin and sew a 1cm seam along the top and bottom edges. You can overlock at this point if you prefer. Press the seams, turn right side out and press again. Repeat for the remaining pillowcase.

I'd be delighted to receive (and give) these as a present.

kantha quilt padded headboard

A simple way to add detail to your bedroom

Like lampshades, you can buy headboard kits in really lovely shapes, complete with instructions and video guidance should you need it. If you want a really simple piece like the one I've made, then you can buy the components and easily put one together in an hour or two.

The balance of hard and soft surfaces is so important for a room to feel right. From a visual point of view, a headboard adds height, which breaks up the long horizontal line of bedside table, bed, bedside table, which in turn anchors the bed in the room.

The choice of fabric is the key to a headboard being either a hideous lump in the room or a thing of beauty. You know that really expensive Colefax & Fowler floral linen that you adore. Well, a set of curtains could be a little eye-watering in price (for good reason), whereas a significantly smaller investment delivers it in headboard form.

I bought the Kantha quilt with *Home Sewn* in mind, as the colour and pattern sat beautifully within the palette I'd planned (see the pinboard on page 142). I wasn't sure what I was going to use it for, but we have a spare room and it needed some focused attention. The spare room is where spare beds reside, isn't it? And they are usually plain and possibly recycled from another life. They contain odd pieces of furniture accumulated when they are no longer fit for purpose anywhere else. It's a normal state of affairs, so don't be alarmed if I've just described your guest bedroom. A bit of effort (maybe some culling) and some beautiful cloth can add the verve and personality the room needs.

You'll need:

9mm plywood cut to size. DIY stores with wood-cutting machines can do this for you. You can choose any height for the headboard but you'll need to have it cut to a specific width to match the bed.

These cutting guides are based on UK bed sizes, so if you have a European or US bed, check the bed size and add 2–3cm for the correct cutting size.

Single – 92cm

Double – 137cm

King – 152cm

Super King – 183cm

Emperor – 203cm

4cm thick upholstery foam to cover one side of the plywood

Upholstery wadding/batting, 10–15cm larger than your plywood all round (upholstery foam and wadding are easily available from eBay).

Enough fabric to wrap around your headboard, plus an extra 20cm in width and height

You'll also need:

Permanent marker

Utility knife

Staple gun

Fabric scissors

Spray adhesive

D-rings, to mount your headboard to the wall

To make:

1 Lay the upholstery foam on a table or clean floor, and then place the plywood on top. Trace the outline of the board onto the foam, then cut the foam with a utility knife.

2 Repeat this process with the wadding but add 10–15cm on all four sides so that you can wrap it over the edge of the plywood when you secure it.

3 Stick the foam to the plywood using spray adhesive (remember to open windows and preferably wear a mask) and let this dry.

4 Spread the wadding out on the table or floor and centre the headboard on top, foam side down. Staple the wadding to the back of the plywood, pulling it taut as you go – this is important.

5 Press your fabric and then place it on the table or floor, right side down. Make sure that it is flat and wrinkle free. Place the headboard on top with the plywood back facing you. If your fabric has a pattern or obvious stripe, take care where you position the headboard, as a slightly off-piste stripe is ever so uncomfortable to look at.

6 Starting at the top centre, working outwards and pulling tightly as you go, staple the fabric to the back of the wood. Then do the bottom edge in the same way, followed by the two sides. When you reach the corners, fold the fabric neatly, as if you were wrapping a present. Once the entire headboard is covered, trim any excess fabric.

7 Attach your headboard to the wall by screwing two D-rings to the back of the plywood and hanging them from screws or hooks in your wall.

To make the purchasing process easier and for a much wider variety of shapes and heights, you can buy a headboard kit. See page 154.

organic voile gathered valance

One for the girls

The swoosh and gather of a cotton gauze valance can elevate the bed to elegance incarnate. Luckily we have a spare bedroom with an antique bed crying out for said flurry. With any spare or guest bedroom, it's the ultimate opportunity to create either hotel-like perfection or the uncompromised bedroom of your dreams. Whilst not all bedrooms (or inhabitants of said bedrooms) come to life with a valance, an antique bed, a fluffy rug and a feminine colour palette positively demand it.

The secret of a successful valance is the fullness of gather and the choice of cloth. Cotton gauze, whilst incredibly cheap, still has a wonderful texture and lightness to it, which works fantastically well when gathered into a floaty froth.

It's also extremely useful and like all my cotton staples can be purchased from a huge variety of suppliers. For *Home Sewn* I tried an Etsy supplier based in India who only sells organic cottons. The quality was excellent and 10 yards was less than the cost of a pair of pillowcases. Cotton gauze has many uses, so any leftovers can be used for a huge variety of projects.

You'll need:

Cotton gauze or voile. For a queen or king-sized bed you will need approximately 8–10m. How much fabric you'll need will depend on the size and height of your bed, as well as how much 'gather' you want. Do your calculations before you order your fabric.

Cotton fabric for the base of the valance. This can be any medium-weight cotton. A valance can sit on a divan base (i.e. under the mattress) or, if your bed is like mine, on the base itself. Measure the base to get the required size and add 3cm to the sides and 4cm to the length. My antique bed is a double, so 135 x 190cm. This meant I needed a piece of fabric 138 x 194cm. You can join fabric together to make the required size or use an old sheet, as you won't see this under the mattress.

Matching cotton thread plus contrasting cotton thread for gathering.

You'll also need:

Iron with steam option

Pins and fabric scissors

Pencil (mechanical is best but a freshly sharpened one will do)

Sewing machine

Long ruler

To make:

1 Measure your bed base, then measure and cut the required fabric for the valance base. On one short end, fold over 1cm and press. Fold over 1cm again, press and sew down. This will be your top edge.

2 Measure and insert a pin at the quarter and halfway points on each of the other three sides – three pins per side.

3 You will add gathered drops to three sides of the base – two long and one short – each sewn on separately. This allows a 'split' at the corners, to fall graciously around legs or posts.

4 Each piece of cotton gauze or voile needs to be a minimum of 2½ times the length of the appropriate base measurement. For fuller gathers you can use up to 3 times the length.

5 Measure the distance from the bed base to the floor. This is the finished height of the valance gathers. To get the correct cutting measurement, also decide if you will hem the gathers. If so, add 4.5cm to the finished height to get the correct cutting measurement. If not, add 1.5cm.

6 You should have several sets of measurements – two lengths (one for the sides and one for the end) and the required height.

7 If, for example, your bed is a double and the base is 40cm from the floor, you might want to hem the gathers, with three times the fullness. You would need to cut 2 x 44.5cm x 5.7m and 1 x 44.5cm x 4.05m. It's easier to cut these as one continuous length down the fabric, rather than cutting across and joining strips. You can, of course, join pieces if necessary.

8 Finish the short edges of each length of gauze. You can overlock, zigzag or turn over a 1cm hem.

9 If you are creating a hem for your valance, start with one side section. Fold over 1cm to the wrong side and press. Fold over a further 2cm and press. Sew the hem in place, sewing close to the edge. Repeat this for the other two pieces.

10 Change your sewing machine to its largest straight stitch setting and replace your top thread with a contrasting coloured thread. On the remaining long raw edge of one piece, sew two parallel lines inside a 1.5cm seam allowance. Leave long threads at both ends and don't backstitch.

11 Fold this piece in half and half again. Press these points. Line these up with the pins on the base cloth and then pin right sides together. This helps you gather the sides evenly.

12 Using your top threads only, pull both ends to create even gathers – it's simple but does take time. Gather one section at a time and once the gathered piece matches the base cloth, pin this securely in place. Once you've gathered and pinned all sections, tie off the threads so that the gathers cannot come undone.

13 Change your sewing machine settings and thread. With the gathering uppermost, sew the pieces together with a 1.5cm seam allowance. Make sure you hold the fabric taut as you sew to prevent folds and tucks forming and slide the pins out as you sew. Then press the seam only – don't press the gathers, as this will flatten them. Finish the seam with a zigzag or overlocker stitch.

14 Repeat for the remaining two sides. Press the base cloth (avoiding the gathers), then find a friend to help lift the mattress and slide this beauty into its rightful place.

linen and cotton velvet curtains

When you need a beautiful curtain but can't or won't do a pinch pleat

Curtains – oh we all want to make these, don't we? I'll confess that I'm not a lover of the overly formal curtain but I do love a swathe of linen as much as the next girl. We have lightweight linen drops in our bedroom so, although I often wake at around 4am in the middle of June, at least I wake up to lovely curtains.

Two winters in though and I thought I'd better get on with making a slightly thicker version. These would be made with the same fixing method – curtain rings and clip hooks, so they are easily changed for the lightweight versions when we slip back into spring. Out came the bolt of never-ending linen – which, to be fair, came to an end after making these. I married it with a thick, grey cotton velvet the same width as the linen for an easy sewing solution.

These curtains are definitely casual in construction, but they have a bit of swagger too. A flipped-over header and a velvet bottom seems to make them feel a bit more than just two pieces of fabric sewn together.

You'll need:

Wide medium-heavy or upholstery-weight linen. Measure the distance from the curtain pole to the floor, then take off approximately 15cm. This is the length you need to cut per panel. To work out the number of panels, measure the length of the curtain pole and multiply this by 1.5. This is the minimum width. Err on the side of generosity, so if your calculations say you need 2.45 drops, just make three drops and revel in the extra folds.

Wide medium/heavy- or upholstery-weight cotton velvet. This needs to be the same width or wider than the linen. Divide the linen length measurement in half to get the required velvet measurement. Trim off any excess width.

Matching cotton thread

You'll also need:

Iron with steam option

Pins and fabric scissors

Long metal ruler

Tailor's chalk or dressmaker's pencil

Sewing machine

Pressing cloth

You'll also need to invest in a curtain pole set and curtain rings with clip hooks if you don't have this fixing method already.

To make:

1 Measure and cut your fabric, then press. Be careful with your iron temperature setting as linen requires a higher setting than cotton velvet. I find placing a towel under the velvet avoids flattening it when you press. Use a pressing cloth, too.

2 With right sides and short edges together, join one panel of linen to one panel of velvet. Use a 1cm seam allowance and zigzag or overlock the seam. Press towards the darker coloured fabric.

3 Turn one long edge over 1cm to the wrong side and press, then repeat. Pin and sew this down, stitching close to the edge. Repeat for the second long edge.

4 Turn one short edge over 1cm to the wrong side and press. Then turn over 3cm, press and sew this down close to the edge of the fold. Repeat for the remaining short edge. Your first panel is complete. Repeat for all remaining panels and then press carefully.

5 Decide where you would like the bottom edge of the curtains to sit – either just touching the floor or pooling slightly. You may need someone to hold the curtain in place whilst you flip the excess to the front of the top of the curtain and clip it in place. Divide the curtain hooks across each panel so that the folds are even.

antique silk scrap
bed bolsters

Not your everyday cushion

You know how easy it is to whip up a cushion – at its very simplest, two pieces of fabric sewn together, an insert stuffed within and a quick slipstitch to close. It's the cheese-on-toast of cushion making and there is nothing wrong with that. I've made many of these and all the others aren't much more complicated – a zip closure or an envelope back is about as intricate as it gets. Textile home goods must feel great – smooth or nubbly, silky or fluffy – it doesn't matter as long as it thrills your fingertips. And they must look good – but only to please your own aesthetic.

Knowing that the construction of a cushion is pretty simple, I wanted to make something that wasn't as time-consuming as a quilt, but still took both time and concentration. This isn't to elevate the cushion to an art form, but because sometimes giving ourselves over to a project that requires considerable concentration is good and/or necessary for both hands and mind.

From a visual perspective I wanted something long and skinny – more of a bolster (fancy cushion speak) and I wanted to use a bag of precious silk and cotton scraps that I had saved for *Home Sewn*. Like the chandelier on page 104, I felt these scraps could create something of great beauty. I really like 'crazy' piecing – the Victorian passion that turned tiny scraps into functioning and highly sought-after quilts. Although time-consuming, they aren't technically difficult to make. They are also a really great way of gaining confidence in choosing and matching colours, textures and patterns. So – a scrappy, crazy cushion using really beautiful fabrics it became… and then I promised myself it would be spared from dog-resting duty. I'm pleased to report – so far, so good.

You'll need:

My cushion has a finished size of 25 x 60cm, but of course you can make it any size you like because you are using buckwheat husks as the filling.

A pile of fabric scraps for the front – you can use old clothing or remnants from other projects. You can of course head off to the shops to buy more fabric.

27 x 62cm piece of medium-weight cotton or linen for the back of the cushion

27 x 62cm piece of cotton lining fabric to stabilise the patchwork

52 x 62cm piece of cotton lining fabric for the lining

1 x 50–55cm invisible zip to match the colour of your backing fabric

Matching cotton thread

Buckwheat hulls/husks. A 1kg bag will be ample for this size (supplier listed on page 154).

You'll also need:

Iron with steam option

Pins, needle and fabric scissors

Quilter's rotary cutter

Long ruler or quilter's ruler

Self-healing cutting mat

Tailor's chalk or dressmaker's pencil

Sewing machine with an invisible zipper foot

Kitchen funnel

To make:

1 Press all of the cloth so that you have flat pieces of fabric to work with for the piecing. Make sure that you have washed anything that needs washing first – you know why!

2 Arrange your cushion front fabrics into piles near your cutting mat, so that you can draw from each one easily.

3 Choose your first piece of fabric and, using the rotary cutter and quilter's ruler, cut it to any size and shape you like.

4 Choose a second piece of fabric and cut another shape making sure that one edge is the same length as one edge on the first shape. Sew these first two shapes together, using a narrow seam. Finger press flat and trim if need be. Cut off the loose threads.

Note: If a rotary cutter and quilter's ruler seems to speak a different language to you, just use a pencil, ruler and scissors.

5 Cut a third piece of fabric – making sure one edge is longer than the edge you want to join it to. Sew, finger press and trim. Keep cutting, sewing, turning and trimming, building up a largish pieced cloth. Measure this, trim a straight edge and set aside.

6 Start a second piece of scrap assembly and build it up in the same manner. The second piece needs to have one edge longer than the straight edge of the first. Trim this straight, then join the two pieces together. Use the off-cuts to start a third piece of scrap cloth.

7 Continue with this method, being mindful of the finished size of the cushion. You should end up with a finished piece of at least 29 x 64cm. Carefully press this flat and lay it right side down on a smooth surface.

8 Lay the piece of 27 x 62cm cotton on top and pin, making sure there is no movement from the patchwork underneath. This piece of cotton will stabilise the

cushion front, as the patchwork technique can cause a little stretch and flare. Machine or hand baste the two pieces together with a narrow seam.

9 Fold the lining cotton in half widthways (i.e. your piece will be 26 x 62cm). Press, then sew a 1cm seam all the way around leaving a 10cm gap. Trim the corners, then turn right side out. Press again.

10 Fill the cushion inner with buckwheat husks. Nudge the funnel into the opening and pour the husks in this way – otherwise enormous mess guaranteed. You want the bolster to be firm but still have some flexibility. Pin the opening to avoid husks escaping and slipstitch closed.

11 Centre the zip on the long edge of the backing fabric. Mark the start and finish of the zip with pins. Pin the front and back cushion pieces right sides together and sew from the edges to these pins.

12 Open the zip and pin it face down on the right side of the edge of the cushion back, with the zip towards the centre. Change the foot on your sewing machine to the invisible zipper foot. Stitch down the zip starting from the bottom and sew towards the zip pull.

13 Close the zip and then pin it face down over the right side of the cushion front fabric. Open the zip and then stitch from the zip pull towards the bottom. Carefully press this with a very cool iron.

14 Change back to the regular presser foot and open the zip. Pin the cushion front and back right sides together and sew a 1cm seam around the three remaining edges. Trim the corners and overlock or zigzag finish the seams. Turn right side out and press again. Insert the buckwheat cushion, close the zip and you're done.

If you prefer, you can make an envelope back or run with the cheese-on-toast option if zips are impossible.

cotton block-print cherry-stone relaxation pillows

And relax...

I could wax lyrical about these cherry-stone pillows ad infinitum. A completely natural source for easing annoying aches and pains, they have put my hot water bottle into early retirement. I had previously completely ignored cherry-stone pillows due to the less-than-attractive coverings and 'packaging', for want of a better description. Shallow this may be, but it is the truth. I didn't even know you could buy the raw materials and how simple it was to create something so incredibly useful. But now I do and now you can too.

The magic in the stones is that they retain and then slowly release moist heat, or stay cool for a long period. They don't get too hot – water bottle burn is a firmly embedded childhood memory – but they remain above body temperature. They mould and shape to your body and have a lovely weight to them which helps you relax. They are, of course, extremely tactile.

As an ingredient, cherry stones are used as a better alternative to wheat in heat packs, but they can also be used as a really effective cold compress. The stones can be washed up to 40 degrees, don't break down and don't develop that slightly furtive smell. They've been pre-cleaned with water, so no revolting chemicals anywhere either.

To use them effectively, you can either heat them in a 750W microwave for two minutes, or do what I do and plonk them on the radiator. Just be careful not to overheat, otherwise they lose their magic. Alternatively, put them in the freezer for an hour or so and your tired eyes or ankles are sorted too.

Fabric. A finished pillow is 25 x 35cm, so 40cm of 110/120cm-wide cotton will make two outers. You will also need the equivalent amount of cotton to make the pillow liners, but this can be any weight of cloth and you can, of course, use scraps. Cotton fabric is best for the cherry-stone pillows, but you could also use lightweight linen.

1 x 3kg bag of cherry stones will make three cushions in the size suggested/ (supplier listed on page 154)

Matching cotton thread

You'll also need:

Iron with steam option

Pins, needle and fabric scissors

Long ruler or quilter's ruler

Measuring jug

Tailor's chalk or dressmaker's pencil

Sewing machine

To make:

1 Wash your fabric, dry and press. You'll know that some cotton fabrics can shrink and any ethnic fabric may have natural dyes. Plus you'll want to remove any gelatine or chemical size from the fabric, as that would be horrible on your skin.

2 Measure and cut two 27 x 37cm rectangles from the lining fabric, then repeat for the outer cloth.

3 With right sides together, pin and sew the lining pieces together. Sew a 1cm seam in from all four edges, leaving a 10cm gap along one of the long sides. Repeat this for the outer fabric, making sure the opening is in approximately the same place. Press the seams flat, then trim the corners. Turn each pillow shape right side out and press again.

4 Slip the liner inside the outer and line up the two openings. Fill a jug with cherry stones – it needs to be manageable for you to lift and pour. Rest the pillow on a table and use one hand to hold the opening wide. Pour the stones in to a point where the pillow is around three-quarters full. The pillow needs to be flexible but not too floppy.

5 Pin the two openings closed and slipstitch first the liner, then the outer and you're finished.

cotton eiderdown

Weighty dreams

There is something about an eiderdown that is uniquely comforting. Their substantiality and weight seem to compel rest upon you. They were called continental quilts in my childhood years and I remember very clearly the process of making my bed. Sheets top and bottom (sometimes not the pale ones of my dreams), two pillows, a green woollen blanket with the lovely satin edge and then, on the cold nights, the continental quilt and matching frilled cushion. Sadly, eiderdowns are a product of yore and therefore hard to find. The other solution is, of course, to make one and these are as close to the real thing as I think you can make at home.

You'll need:

Single 140 x 200cm feather and down duvet. There are different tog weights available – the higher the number, the thicker and heavier the eiderdown will be. If possible, try to buy one that is sectioned in grids, not rows.

4.5m of wide light–medium-weight cotton or linen fabric at least 1.2m wide. If you are using a narrower width, then add extra for joining, as required. If you want to use a different fabric on each side, you'll need 2.1m of one and 2.4m of the other (the second fabric being used for flat piping). To add even more detail, you can use a third fabric for the piping, so reduce and add fabric lengths accordingly.

Matching cotton thread

Matching (or contrasting) quilting thread

A small scrap of leather or thick woollen cloth

You'll also need:

Iron with steam option

Pins and fabric scissors

Safety pins

Long ruler or quilter's ruler

Tailor's chalk or dressmaker's pencil

Sewing machine

Darning needle

To make:

1 Wash, dry and press the fabric. Cut two pieces at 142 x 202cm. If you need to join fabric to create the required width, it's useful to plan the join to line up with the duvet joins. They are straight lines or grids. I used a grid-based duvet, so took these measurements and made sure the join line of the fabric matched up to this line. If this seems maddeningly difficult, don't worry. Press any seams.

2 Cut the remainder of the fabric into 3cm strips. Sew the strips together end to end until you have a piece at least 7m in length. Fold the strip in half to create 1.5cm wide flat piping and press with a steam iron.

3 Pin the flat piping to the right side of one of the flat panels, raw edge to raw edge. Leave about 5–10cm of the piping strip free. Using your sewing machine, baste stitch the piping to the panel approximately 5mm in. Ease the strip around corners. When you get near the beginning, backstitch and remove from the sewing machine. Trim the excess piping, leaving around 1cm. Fold and pin the piping under itself and slipstitch down. Press the piping flat.

4 Pin the two panels right sides together. Sew them together, starting 30cm in from the end of one of the short edges. When you reach this short edge again, sew along it to 30cm from the corner. This will leave a gap for you to feed the duvet through. Press the seams open, then flatten and clip the corners. Turn right side out and press again.

5 Clear a clean floor space that is larger than the duvet. Carefully feed the duvet inside the eiderdown cover, making sure you spread it evenly corner to corner. Use the safety pins to hook the corner of the duvet to each corner of the cover. Give the eiderdown a shake to spread the layers out and then lay it flat.

6 Now this bit is a little fiddly. You need to decide a grid or line formation on which to place the leather/wool 'buttons'. It's easier to line them up with the preformed pockets in the duvet, but you need to make sure the duvet remains flat. Use safety pins to push through all the layers and create your grid.

7 Cut out the required number of 'buttons'. Use a coin to trace directly onto the leather/wool. Thread the darning needle with a double thickness of quilting thread. Push the needle through the back of one of the safety pin points. Remove the safety pin once the thread is knotted and secure. Then push the needle through a leather button and back down through the eiderdown. Repeat a few times until it's nice and secure. Thread to the back of the eiderdown, tie off and trim the thread. Repeat for all remaining points. Check that both sides of the fabric remain flat as you go. Remove the four safety pins from the corners.

8 Pin the remaining edge close. Either hand slipstitch or machine sew the seam closed.

eating & sharing

cotton, silk and leather chandelier

A bit of magic from a few scraps

I hope that you've made or earmarked some thing(s) to make from *Home Sewn*. Perhaps you're already drying your hands on freshly sewn tea towels or setting your coffee cup down on the sartorially elegant coaster of your dreams (or maybe it's just me that dreams of such things). But whatever you've made, you'll have some scraps – and scraps, well, they can be beautiful.

I think it's important to make something that pleases you just for the sake of it, like the butterfly wall I adore (on page 32) – utterly purposeless but lovely to look at. What we choose to make and fill our homes with should nurture us as well as be functional. Most of the projects in *Home Sewn* fulfil a real need, but one or two of them – they're just for fun.

So from snippets and odds and ends you can make a fabric chandelier, using up precious pieces of cloth and ephemera, as well as a bit of liquid gilt and metallic thread. Its sole point of existence is simply to be beautiful to look at – how delightful.

1 lampshade ring (the ring without the bulb fitting – you can use the other ring to make the pendant shade) or strong wire

Scraps of fabric

Cotton or metallic thread

Liquid gilt or metallic paint

Thread, ribbon or string to hang the chandelier

You'll also need:

Pencil (mechanical is best but a freshly sharpened one will do)

Sewing machine

Fabric scissors

A small circular object(s) about 4–5cm in diameter to trace around – a paint pot, bud vase or tiny espresso cup would be perfect

Small paintbrushes

Pliers, if making your own ring from wire

To make:

1 My instructions should be used as a starting point only, as the chandelier is very simple to put together and elaborate on. You can create larger, smaller or multi-tiered options. You could forget the ring and make garlands or curtain drops (70s flashback). Make it pink, black or floral, or load it up with ephemera – just use what you have and enjoy the process of making.

2 If using wire, make a ring – any size you fancy – and twist it closed with pliers. Then paint the ring using liquid gilt or metallic paint (or any paint really).

3 Whilst the ring is drying, you can trace and cut the circles. A rummage through your kitchen cupboards will find something to use as a template. You can have more than one size and I'm sure I don't need to tell you that you can trace any shape you want – you'll see a few sneaky butterflies on mine. Then cut out the fabric and line up the shapes, sizes or colours in piles. You can paint any of the shapes with gilt or paint (just thought about the glitter option and wish I'd thought of that before…).

4 Before you start sewing, make sure you have an end of thread around 15–20cm long at the start of each drop. You'll need this to tie each drop onto the ring.

5 To create a drop, use a straight stitch on your sewing machine and sew through the centre of a circle. Then feed a second circle through and on until you have the length you would like. You don't need to backstitch, but leave a small gap between each circle. When you get to the last circle, backstitch, then leave a tail of thread.

6 Repeat until you have as many drops as you want/ need/have time for. Tie each drop to the ring, being careful not to tangle them. Finally, tie three pieces of thread, ribbon or string to the ring and hang the chandelier from your chosen point. You can trim the excess thread from the bottom of each drop, tie gathered ephemera to them or leave the threads dangling.

organic linen tea towels

Everyday mess can still be beautiful — or why you need good tea towels

Quite frankly, my tea towels were (and some still are) a disgrace: tatty, too small and often sartorially challenged. The purchase of marvellous — read expensive — organically dyed linen replacements always fell by the wayside when considered next to other kitchen purchase options. Ask yourself, if you had a significant sum to spend on kitchen goodies, are you going to buy an Italian pasta maker or four tea towels? For me, there really isn't a question to answer. However, with just over one metre of high-quality linen, you can make the same four tea towels, using very limited sewing skills and a lot less outlay.

You could eke out even more tea towels from old (but robust) linen sheets for a similar cost.

From a form and function point of view, most tea towels that you buy are made of cotton and these simply don't do as good a job as linen. Linen is perfect for the job of drying and absorbing. It's non-allergenic and anti-bacterial — excellent properties for removing water from eating vessels. It's also very strong and stronger wet than dry — also excellent qualities. It can take on a lot of water before it feels wet and dries remarkably quickly. It's a lint-free option which, if you have ever been served a glass of wine with a floater of fluff in it, you'll appreciate this point. And it resists dirt and stains. All in all, absolutely perfect for the job.

From an aesthetic point of view — linen is just wonderful to handle and comes in really lovely colours and weights. With a couple of hours of cutting, pressing and sewing, your kitchen linen will rival that of the finest kitchen stores across the land.

When I was planning and purchasing all the fabric for *Home Sewn*, I came across a bolt of Irish linen. It's so fantastic you'll see it popping up in lots of the projects. Not just because it's beautiful, but also because it works.

You'll need:

1.1–1.2m of 140cm-wide linen will make four tea towels. Choose a medium-weight linen rather than a fine or heavy weight. Fine linen won't perform well enough and thick linen will make these difficult to sew at the corners. If your fabric is a narrower width (usually 120cm), then you will need 1.4m. You can also use a vintage linen sheet, but make sure that it isn't worn or too thick.

Your tea towels don't have to be a precise size but somewhere between 50/55 x 65/70cm is great – any larger and they become unwieldy. Your cut size will need to be 4cm wider and longer than your finished size, so either start with your desired finished size and work backwards, or work with the piece of fabric you have to hand.

Matching thread (or contrasting if you prefer)

You'll also need:

Iron with steam option

Pins and fabric scissors

Metal ruler

Sewing machine

Pressing cloth (a large, damp piece of scrap cotton or linen)

To make:

1 Start by washing your linen. This is to ensure there is no dye run and to remove any (although there should be very little) shrinkage. Iron your linen using a steam iron. At this stage just glide the iron across to remove wrinkles.

2 Remove the selvedge from both edges of your fabric. Fold the fabric in half lengthways so that you line up the outside edges. Then press along the fold line.

3 Check your cut edges (the top and bottom edges) to see if they line up. Sometimes fabric stores don't cut perfectly, or have cut a sample piece (who doesn't love collecting fabric samples...) leaving a skew or wobbly edge. Use a long metal ruler to draw a straight line across each edge at right angles to the outside edges, then trim away the excess. You can use a rotary cutter to make quick work of this.

4 Cut the fabric in half along the pressed fold line. Fold each piece in half again, top to bottom, and press. Cut these pieces along the fold line and you have four tea towel-shaped pieces of cloth to complete.

5 Linen often doesn't have a right or wrong side, but if your fabric has a pattern or weave on the right side, make sure you turn the fabric to the wrong side in the following steps.

6 With your first piece of fabric, turn the top edge over 1cm and, using a hot steam iron, press. You will need to use a pressing cloth as linen can become shiny if you use a steam iron directly on it. Rather than sliding the iron up and down, you need to place the iron on the fabric, press down, lift up, move along and press down again. Let the fabric cool before you move it off the ironing board and then repeat this for the bottom edge.

7 Turn the first side edge over 1cm and repeat the above. Repeat with the second side. Then repeat the whole process so that you have turned each edge over twice, so no raw edges are on show. Your corners will have four layers of fabric, thus the need for a medium-weight cloth!

8 Pin and sew the edges down with the wrong side facing you. Sew just within 1cm so that you are catching the edge of the hem. When you reach a corner, make sure your needle will sew through the layers. Sometimes you may need to hand-guide your needle through. To do this, pretend you are using your grandmother's treadle machine and rather than using your foot control, just hand-turn the balance wheel (the round thing on the right) to move the needle up and down.

9 Remove the pins, press again and you're done.

To speed through your tea towel-making session, I suggest you create a production line – press all of the fabric pieces, then pin, then sew them all at the same time.

An inexpensive but incredibly tasteful way to give your home some rugs

hand-painted canvas floor cloth

You may ask yourself – 'what is a floor cloth'? Don't worry, I didn't know what they were either. I had seen them but ignored them, as they can be a little challenging on the aesthetic front. Floor cloths have been around since the eighteenth century and were popular across all classes and countries. They were useful alternatives to rugs and carpets, or used to emulate tiled or stone floors. They were (and still are) simply a painted piece of canvas art.

A chance encounter with an old one that was vaguely stylish – spattered, if you please – and I realised this is a great textile project. It's definitely useful and can be beautiful if one avoids over zealous stencils.

In winter I have a beautiful antique carpet in the studio, anchoring our writing table. In summer this gets rolled up and put away but then the table looked a little sad and unanchored. I thought of a sisal or sea grass rug, but then I thought about pins – and that was the end of that particular sartorial daydream. So the solution had to be flat as well as functional, attractive and inexpensive. I also had a mountain of canvas and some leftover paint, so all the materials and tools were in place. I like a mixture of precision and handmade in everything I design and make, so a hand-painted chevron shape was perfect as it can be both sharp and a little wobbly.

You'll need:

Heavy-weight canvas. Canvas is measured in ounces so you want 12oz or 15oz as a minimum weight. The amount of fabric you need will depend on the size of the rug you would like. Add 12cm to the width and length of the finished size to get the correct amount of fabric to purchase.

Matching cotton thread

2 x 750ml cans of acrylic wall paint, in the colours of your choice. You can use leftover wall emulsion rather than buying something new.

1 x 750ml can of water-based undercoat or primer/undercoat. Match the colour to the strength of colours you are using as the topcoats. If the paints are contrasting in tone, use a lighter based undercoat.

1 x 750ml can (or spray can) of water-based clear acrylic or polyurethane varnish

2 x 5cm paintbrushes

You'll also need:

Iron with steam option

Pins and fabric scissors

Pencil (mechanical is best but a freshly sharpened one will do)

Sewing machine

Decorator's dustsheets

Decorator's tape

Quilter's ruler. 15 x 30cm will work best, or a 45-degree set square and ruler can be used.

To make:

1 Cut the fabric to your desired size, remembering to add an extra 12cm. It's best to make mitred corners for a floor cloth rather than the simpler tea towel and napkin method. It will be neater, longer lasting and – with thicker fabric – achievable to sew on a domestic sewing machine.

2 Use the pencil to mark a line 4cm in from all four edges. Then press two opposite edges in 2cm to meet the pencilled lines. Fold these over another 4cm to encase the raw edges. Press, then pin the folded edges. Stitch them into place, sewing close to the edge. Make sure you start and stop within the intersecting drawn line, so that you are able to fold the remaining two edges.

3 Repeat for the remaining two edges. Then fold all corners into a triangle shape and press. Slipstitch or machine stitch the corners closed.

4 Clear a table or floor space that is larger than your floor cloth and that you can keep small and four-legged visitors away from. Lay down the dustsheet and make sure it is taut, using the decorator's tape if necessary.

Note: for the ease of demonstrating, I went against this advice and used my lovely table – no damage, but don't take the risk yourself. Lay the floor cloth flat on top and straighten.

5 Paint the floor cloth with a coat of primer/undercoat and leave to dry. Repeat with a second coat and leave to dry. For added durability you can prime the underside also. If so, do this first so that you don't have to keep flipping the floor cloth over. Once dry, paint the cloth in your first colour – the lightest tone. Apply a second coat if using your floor cloth in a heavy use area.

6 If your rug is rectangular, decide which direction you want the chevrons to run. With a pencil, mark the centre point. Use the quilter's ruler or set square to create the chevron pattern, by drawing a 45-degree triangle centred off this pencil mark. This first triangle needs to be 5cm or less in depth. Move the ruler down 5cm and create another triangle. Move across and down the cloth creating chevrons, being careful not to 'skew' your lines. It sounds tricky, but it isn't once you get into the swing of it.

7 Now for the freestyle chevrons – which I love. Using a 5cm brush and the second paint colour, paint every second chevron row. I start in a corner and brush away as this gives a cleaner edge without being too crisp. Don't overload the paintbrush – it's better to paint twice than have a blobby corner. Work your way across and down. Leave to dry. You can paint a second coat if you wish but I like the slight transparency.

8 The final step is to apply a minimum of two coats of varnish. It's important that you leave each coat to dry for the required time, otherwise your floor cloth won't be properly protected.

You can also apply two coats to the underside of the cloth if you want to be able to clean both sides. Clean your floor cloths with a little detergent and water, as you would clean a painted canvas.

Last but important point, if you are placing the floor cloth in an open space (i.e. with nothing to anchor it), make sure you have carpet/rug grips or a non-slip pad underneath.

cotton voile stamped café curtains

When you need a little privacy, you don't need to forsake beauty

One of the great pleasures of having a window above your kitchen bench is the ability to see out and therefore connect with your surroundings. This is positively idyllic when faced with rolling hills, your children playing or a great cityscape. However, if your view is a wall or a block of flats is looking back at you, perhaps you need a little privacy, a little beauty in front of you or fabric to shield you from something that isn't beautiful.

My nana and grandma had café curtains in their kitchens. In the heat of a New Zealand summer they were essential to keep the sun off the food and screen the not-so-attractive backyard goings-on. Café curtains were a simple solution to a real need. And I do suggest that you make them only if you need to – don't hang them at a window if you have that amazing view, because decoration for decoration's sake is silly.

Of course these simple curtains can be used to fulfil a wide range of privacy needs. We have a garden room at home where the doors are made from glass. Lovely it is, but sometimes it is pressed into providing extra sleeping quarters. To ensure guests have their privacy I made a set of café curtains, placed a set of hooks on the doors and a spare room was born. When guests leave, I simply remove the curtains, roll them up and tuck them back into the linen cupboard. A simple solution that is both useful and beautiful.

Cotton voile is another wonderful cloth that can be used across a huge variety of projects. It's available from those wonderful suppliers of cotton canvas, but you also have a few more purchasing choices. It's best in plain white or unbleached and will be available in widths of 90–140cm. It lets light in but isn't see-through – marvellous stuff. Often woven in India, you can find delightful hand-loomed and/or organic versions that have a palpable feel of the handmade. The cheaper, mass-produced versions are often coated in a gelatine or chemical size, which makes the fabric feel a little stiff. Once washed, it softens considerably. If it's particularly cheap, it will also shrink considerably. Once you find a version you like to work with, it's a good cloth to have a stockpile of – mind you, I think that about most fabric…

You'll need:

Cotton voile. Measure the space that your curtain will hang from. You will need twice the width and 7cm more than the height. If your hanging space is shorter than the width of the cloth, you can use the fabric horizontally rather than having to join widths.

1 curtain wire set, or curtain wire and a packet of metal screw hooks and eyes. It usually comes in 2, 5 or 15m lengths.

Wooden blocks (see the supplier suggestions on page 153)

Fabric ink or stamp

Matching cotton thread

You'll also need:

Iron with steam option

Pins and fabric scissors

Sewing machine

Domestic pliers

Decorator's dustsheet

To make:

1 Wash, dry, then press the voile.

2 Screw the metal eyes into the window, door or cupboard frame where your curtain will hang. Measure between these points – twice for accuracy – for the desired width and double the measurement. Measure the desired height of the curtain and add 7cm. You may need to join panels to get the desired width, so for each join add 2cm to get the correct widths. Cut your fabric.

3 Join the fabric panels if necessary, with a 1cm seam. Finish the edges with either a simple zigzag stitch, a French seam if you prefer a refined finish, or whizz it through your overlocker if you have one. Press.

4 Turn over 1cm on the top edge and press. Turn over a further 2cm and press. Sew this in place close to the edge. Repeat for the bottom edge turning 1cm, then 3cm. Press the curtain panel(s).

5 Turn over 1cm on the top edge and press. Turn over a further 2cm and press. Sew this in place close to the edge. Repeat for the bottom edge turning 1cm, then 3cm. Press the curtain panel(s).

6 Protect a table or floor with the dustsheet and lay the curtain on top, making sure it's wrinkle free. Just a little stamping to do now! After a few practice presses, simply ink your blocks and stamp your curtain as much or as little as you want. You can preplan a pattern or go freestyle.

7 Whilst the fabric is drying, use the pliers to cut the curtain wire. Take 10 per cent off the original width measurement as this ensures the curtain will stay taut when hanging. Screw one hook into each end of the wire.

8 Once dry, thread the curtain onto the wire, then stretch it onto the eyes – and you're done.

storytelling canvas
tablecloth

A narrative of silver and gold

Laying the table with a cloth is an excellent opportunity to create a piece of art, tell a story or simply to celebrate an important person or occasion. Whether for Christmas or a significant birthday, a piece of fabric, some paint and a few bits of crockery can create something quite extraordinary.

In my arsenal of utility cloth is cotton calico. It's another staple that I buy in bulk, because I use it for so many things and it is really good value. It's excellent lining, backing and sampling cloth, and is perfect for a myriad of home staples. It's natural, can be organic and of course comes in many widths. It is therefore absolutely perfect to make a disposable tablecloth for a party or event.

With this project I thought I'd tell the story of a party that's already passed – a gilded, shiny party where the table was full and much fun was had – recreating the spillages of a great dinner but using metallic paint. Imagine copper wine dribbles and silvery water tumbles. Of course, by the end of the evening these metallic 'stains' will be joined by the real thing – but who cares, it's a one-use piece of frivolity and that is completely the point of it.

For my party tale, I used a mixture of silver, copper and warm gold paint. My tablecloth can't be washed, so use fabric paint instead if you'd like to re-use it. I think that three colours work best, but it can be any combination of colours to fit your style or the occasion. To create the party 'stains' I used a mixture of dinner plates, wine bottles, wine and champagne glasses, water tumblers, jugs and pudding plates – everything in fact you'd have at a party.

You'll need:

Natural cotton calico fabric. To work out the correct amount of fabric, measure your table and add a minimum of 65cm to the width and length. This will give you a nice amount of overhang. There's nothing worse than a flappy tablecloth – they look truly uncomfortable. You can, of course, go as wide and long as you like – pool onto the floor if that's the look you're after. Calico comes in a wide variety of widths from 120 to 305cm, so every table size and creative concept is covered.

Matching cotton thread

Metallic paint, liquid gilt or fabric paint

You'll also need:

Iron with steam option

Pins and fabric scissors

Sewing machine

Decorator's dustsheet(s), make sure you have a plastic one for this project

A set of small paintbrushes

A collection of plates, bottles, glasses and cups. They each need to have a ridged bottom so that you can use them like a stamp

Cloths/water and plastic bowls for preparing and cleaning the above

To make:

1 Wash the calico and press with a steam iron once dry. If you want to hem your tablecloth (you don't have to), then turn each edge over 2cm and press, using a hot steam iron. Rather than sliding the iron up and down, you need to place the iron on the fabric, press down, lift up, move along and press down again (the same method as the tea towels and napkins). Repeat this, turning over 3cm and press again. Sew the hems down, stitching close to the edge. Press again.

2 Lay the dustsheets on your work surface and the surrounding area. Make sure that everything that needs to be protected is completely covered. As you will be pressing paint onto the tablecloth, lay it on top of the plastic dustsheet making sure that your table is completely protected.

3 Plan out your table setting – how many places there will be and where any candlesticks, vases, etc. will sit on the table once you have completed your party tableau.

4 Start with the dinner plate markings. Choose a paint colour, then paint a liberal amount of paint on the under rim of the plate. Choose your spot, then firmly place the plate painted side down onto the tablecloth. Try not to drag the plate or wrinkle the cloth. Lift up cleanly and you've made the first mark. Continue around the table until you have completed all the plate markings. Clean the plate to remove all the paint.

5 Continue painting and placing your glasses, jugs and bowl marks, mixing your colours as you choose. Make sure you clean everything once you have finished with it – paint is not edible…

6 Finish your tablecloth with a liberal sprinkling of painterly dribbles. Carefully flick or shake your laden brush around other markings and down the sides of the cloth.

7 Let the cloth dry and then loosely fold it if you need to put it away before the event.

8 A nice addition would be to write and sign the tablecloth at the party. What a wonderful way to remember the event! Just remember to protect the table underneath if you're using paint or indelible markers.

cotton canvas storage containers

And of course you'll need good storage solutions

I'm not fanatically tidy, but I do find it dismal when your home turns into a dumping ground for detritus. It creates emotional chaos and it is really very tiresome wading through piles of stuff when you don't need to. I don't think you should create more storage in order to have 'more' but the necessary everyday stuff of life is often awkward and fiddly, so needs sorting. I don't want to think about these humdrum parts of life more than I need to (sorting paper, anyone?), so I have the preserving jars and resealable containers for food and other small stuff. However I didn't have that last layer sorted – the newspapers, teenagers' sports kit and rope/string collections, to name but a few.

So I thought I'd design something that would sort these essential but awkward things and needs begat these. Essential to the design solution is a flat base. I didn't want to make anything that had to lean on something else to stay standing – that's just annoying. A few size options were vital and they needed to have an easy open/close solution – I don't want to wrangle with my root veg or other people's muddy socks. Finally, as this is yet another functional product, the making wasn't going to take more than an afternoon.

I've now made scores of these containers. They hold everything from dog paraphernalia, clothing and aforementioned root veg to fabric scraps in my work studio. Although they are not the most visually enchanting or technically challenging project, they are a totally useful piece of kit that you'll use over and over in your own home. I can't think of a better reason to make them.

Shall we discuss cotton canvas (sometimes called cotton duck – quack)? It's fantastic stuff. It comes in useful cloth weights and extremely wide widths; it's utilitarian and rather attractive. The high-five moment is the price – tremendously reasonable verging on very cheap if you buy in bulk. The secret is to buy cotton canvas from art framers or 'basic' fabric suppliers. These retailers just specialise in the essential everyday cloths and so can keep their prices lower. (Of course, suppliers are listed for you at the back of the book.) You can purchase organic versions if you prefer and can source canvas you know has been grown with people and planet in mind as much as profit. It's brilliant cloth and you'll find it popping up all the way through *Home Sewn* for both its versatility and rugged good looks.

You'll need:

1.5m of wide canvas will make one container of each size or two of the large size. However, this is the kind of fabric I'd suggest buying at least 5m of as it will always be useful. You'll also need to think about the weight of canvas you want to use. The heavier the canvas, the more rigid the container. This is great on the larger sizes but may prove unwieldy for the smallest. You also need to make sure your domestic machine can sew through several layers of the fabric. Note that waxed canvas won't be suitable for these containers if you want to wash them. Waxed canvas can only be wiped clean and prefers not to be in contact with an iron – the voice of experience...

1.5–2m of lining fabric. The length you need depends on the width of the fabric. If you are using 110-120cm–wide fabric you'll need 2m. If using a wider width fabric (usually around 140cm), then 1.5m will be ample. You can use up any old fabric you have or choose something new. Think about a washable waterproof lining for storing produce (also teenagers' sports kit).

1 packet of sash cord (available from your local DIY store) or a few metres of rope, 5-7mm diameter

Matching thread

1-2 packets of 11mm eyelets. You'll need a minimum of 8 eyelets for the large, 6 for the medium and 4 for the small container. The eyelets will come with the tools needed to fix them to the fabric and they are easy to find at haberdashery stores or online.

You'll also need:

Iron with steam option

Pins and scissors

Long ruler or quilter's ruler

Pencil (mechanical is best but a freshly sharpened one will do)

Small hammer

Sewing machine

Paper scissors

Sellotape/ sticky tape or paperglue

Finished size:

Large: 34 x 59cm (width x height)

Medium: 27 x 49cm (width x height)

Small: 20 x 31cm (width x height)

To make:

1 Go to www.cassandraellis/homesewn and download the pdf pattern file marked 'Storage Container'. This is delivered as a print-at-home pattern so you'll just need access to an A4 or US letter printer. You'll also need paper scissors and either sellotape/stickytape or paper glue. All other information is provided on the pdf file – oohh exciting!

2 For every container, you need to cut one body and one bottom in the canvas fabric, and the same in the lining fabric.

3 Start with your lining. Pin the two short ends of the body together, right sides facing, then sew a 1cm seam. Press the seam flat, then open. Take care with the temperature of the iron if you are using waterproof fabric as it will have a lower heat threshold. You'll now have a tube shape to work with.

4 With your right sides together, pin the bottom circle to one end of the tube – either end is fine. With the circle uppermost on your machine, carefully sew a 1cm seam. As you're sewing a curve you may need to encourage the circle to stretch slightly. You can baste this seam first if you prefer to remove the possibility of bunching and therefore unpicking. Press the seam flat, then clip. This helps the seam sit nicely – good seam!

5 Repeat for the cotton canvas outer, increasing the heat and using the steam option for lovely flat seams. Before you join the body to the bottom, you may want to topstitch along the body seam. It isn't necessary if this seems too much design thought for an onion bag!

6 Turn the canvas outer right side out and slip it inside the lining, which will be wrong side out. Pin the top edges together and sew a 1cm seam, leaving a 10cm gap. Press this seam, again being careful with your temperature setting. Pull the canvas outer through the gap and push the lining inside the outer. Press the top edge again.

>>>

<<< 7 Pin the gap and topstitch all the way round 2mm from the edge. Topstitch a second row 10mm in, then remove the pins. Press one last time.

8 Decide how many eyelets you want to use on your container. To insert the eyelets, use a pencil to mark between 4, 6, 8 or 10 dots evenly spread, 7cm from the top edge of the container. You don't have to be exact, but do try to be fairly even. How many eyelets you choose depends on the look you want for the finished container and the size you are making. As long as you have an even number of eyelets, the rest is creativity.

9 Unless you've used eyelets before, I would 'waste' one by practising on a spare piece of cloth. The eyelets come with instructions, but a bit of physical doing will make it a lot easier to understand and settles the nerves. I always stand at a table when I make eyelet holes and it's best to use something like a chopping board or old magazine underneath to avoid any furniture damage. Follow the instructions on the packet, centring the eyelet hole on your pencil mark. If you don't want to use eyelets, you can just make a series of belt loops to hold the rope – it won't be as robust, but if it's socks and not onions being stored, this won't matter.

10 Once you have created all the eyelets (or loops), then cut a length of rope and thread it through the eyelet holes. The length depends on whether the storage bags will be hanging, carried, etc. – it won't be difficult for you to work out what you need.

khadi cotton lap napkins

And then came napkins...

Definitely more sartorially elevated in our kitchen cupboards are fabric napkins. They can also be an expensive investment, but considering how simple/identical to tea towels they are to construct, they are another practical, yet satisfying item to make.

The secret to a good napkin is firstly the fabric. Linen and hemp are best for all of the same reasons as for tea towels. My magnificent 15-year-old hemp napkins are unstained and hole free, with the added advantage of unbelievable softness after many washes. Although investment in the fabric can be expensive, they will last and are excellent everyday staples.

Cotton napkins can also make a rather lovely addition to your napkin supply. Cotton comes in a plethora of colours and patterns, as well as offering a lower fabric cost option to linen. You can rustle up four unique block-printed cotton napkins for around the same cost as buying just one – which is certainly a very good incentive to make lots of them.

The second secret is size. Again, commercial napkins can be a little teensy – it's like wearing a too-short skirt when your napkin barely covers your lap – unduly uncomfortable.

And the third secret – well, that's all about aesthetic pleasure. I don't think there is a more uplifting supper table than bare wood, gleaming cutlery, clear glass and lovely napkins – simple but special. It means your supermarket curry for two can be just as special an eating experience as a dinner party for eight. I feel that's reason enough to make and use them on a daily basis, don't you?

Weirdly, although napkins and tea towels are ostensibly the same thing and made in the same way – one is eminently suitable as a gift and the other most definitely is not. I'm sure you know which is which.

I've used two different khadi cottons for these napkins – hand woven loveliness in a good medium weight. Although they are blue, they aren't dyed in indigo, because that could be an on-going dye-leak disaster. It's important with napkins that the colour doesn't run for obvious reasons. Any moisture contact means unfixed colour will run. So choose cotton, linen or hemp that you know is colour-fast. If you're not sure, boil it in some water with salt as a fixative and then wash again. If there is still dye run, redirect the fabric towards a useful life as a cushion cover.

You'll need:

1.1–1.2m of 120cm-wide cotton will make four napkins. Linen and hemp are often wider as are some cottons, but annoyingly not quite wide enough to get three napkins across. For ample lap coverage, your napkins need to be 50cm square-ish as a minimum, although you can make them up to around 60cm square. They don't have to be a perfect square either. Rather than waste fabric, you can make them rectangular in shape (looks like a tea towel, but isn't).

Choose a medium-weight fabric rather than a fine or heavy weight. Your fabric can be old or new but it does need to be a natural fibre. And if you are making these as a gift, I always think eight is the right number. Six doesn't allow for last-minute guests or ample washing changeover and eight, well it just feels on the right side of generous.

Matching thread (or contrasting if you prefer)

You'll also need:

Iron with steam option

Pins and fabric scissors

Metal ruler

Sewing machine

Pressing cloth

To make:

1 Well – this is rather simple. You just make them in exactly the same method as the tea towels on page 108. That's it. It's projects such as these that make you question why you ever bought the finished product in the first place…

leather placemats
and coasters

Protecting precious surfaces – without resorting to ugly solutions

For me aesthetics and practical needs are prioritised equally. Whilst it's simple to craft or purchase beautiful cushions and curtains, the small functional textiles of home (remember tea towels?) often go awry or are ridiculously expensive. I needed coasters to protect our tables at home, but couldn't find any that were visually appealing and/or affordable – and so I was stumped. There is no point in purchasing something that you're unhappy to look at (we would never do it with clothing), so I did without, but this was not a long-term solution either.

The 'aha' moment came when I wasn't thinking about my coaster issues. Whilst designing another project using leather, I had sample scraps lying on my workbench and sitting next to it was a mug of tea. The mug was handmade porcelain and rather beautiful – the leather a rather fine shade of old gold. I put the mug on said scrap of leather because it looked nice… admired it for a moment and realised my problem was solved. Robust and handsome leather was the perfect solution to this irksome issue. Simple to source and make, leather also looks better with age, so marks would not be a problem. They are also heat resistant, attractive and fit for purpose, which fits nicely into my 'useful and beautiful' mantra.

You'll need:

Leather. You can use any kind you like, but it should be a minimum of 1.2mm thick. Don't go too thick (as in saddle leather), as this will prove almost impossible to cut with domestic equipment. How much you need will depend on how many and what size coasters you want to make.

You'll also need:

Fabric scissors

Paper scissors

Pattern-making paper or greaseproof paper

A selection of glasses and small plates to use as templates

Two pencils (mechanical or sharp for paper and soft lead for leather)

To make:

1 Embarrassingly simple really. Decide what you would like the coasters for – maybe just mugs and glasses, maybe a whole table extravaganza. Each coaster needs to be bigger than the bottom of the vessel resting on it. Just select bowls or plates – anything round really – to create the sizes you need. For cups and glasses I used the rim of a small bowl and for dinner plates I used a side plate as a template.

2 Trace around the shapes onto the paper, then cut the patterns out. As leather is neither square nor perfect, move the paper shapes around the hides to get the maximum number of coasters. Both types of paper are slightly translucent so will allow you to see any blemishes or holes. You can skip this step and trace directly from bowl to leather if you prefer.

3 Using a very sharp pair of scissors, cut around each shape in long smooth cuts, keeping just inside the tracing line.

4 That's it really – a very simple sartorial solution to a small but irritating issue.

organic cotton loose chair covers

What to do with a fragile and/or ugly chair

I have a pair of wooden chairs that are on their last legs — literally. They aren't antiques nor restoration-worthy as they are pedigree-free and quite plain in the looks department. They are however very important to me, so I will keep them until they collapse into a heap. This fragility means they really shouldn't be sat on, so I use them on photo shoots (I'll carry it!!!!) or as a bedside table in our spare room. They get repainted often — currently Farrow & Ball Calamine — and I know that they will give me great pleasure until that fateful day when they crumple into a pile of sticks.

Making a simple slipcover hides the ugly and elevates the fragile to a different place, but you may also have some rather attractive wooden chairs that could do with a little slipcover now and then. Perhaps you have too much 'hard' and not enough 'soft' in a room. Textiles are necessary to visually and emotionally balance out all the solid surfaces, otherwise our rooms can feel a little bleak and clinical.

These slipcovers aren't a precise upholstery project, rather a more liberated idea that also gives you some practice at pattern making. For me, it's to keep my chairs together and relevant to how my home looks now.

I made the slipcovers for my chairs from the never-ending bolt of linen. One chair is now sitting in my studio, looking rather fine and almost spry, its pink legs poking out of a rumpled yet tactile coat. I still won't sit on it, but as inanimate objects go, it seems to have life flowing through it.

You'll need:

A chair. A simple armless wooden chair is best. It can have a rounded or square top.

Fabric of your choice. A simple chair uses approximately 1–1.25m of 140cm-wide fabric.

Matching cotton thread

Embroidery thread (not compulsory)

You'll also need:

Iron with steam option

Pins and fabric scissors

Paper scissors

Sewing machine

Embroidery needle (not compulsory)

Pattern-making paper

Pencil with soft lead

To make:

1 Wash your fabric. You need to remove any shrinkage before you make the slipcover or you'll end up with one-size-too-small issues. Press your fabric and set aside.

2 Lay the pattern paper flat on a clean table or floor. Lay the chair on top of the paper, back side down. Trace around the back of the chair, adding approximately 3–4cm all around. Cut this shape out roughly. Chairs are usually symmetrical, so fold the paper shape in half and even out your tracing marks, erring on the generous side. Check against the chair, make any adjustments and cut this final shape as a pattern for the front and back of the cover.

3 Lay the fabric flat, then fold in half and pin the pattern piece to it. You can shuffle the fabric fold so that you don't waste any cloth. Cut two.

4 With right sides together, pin and sew the pieces together using a 1cm seam allowance, leaving the bottom edge open. You need to leave a 1cm gap at the beginning and end of this seam so that you can attach the seat and skirt. Press the seams flat, then open. If using wool or linen, remember to use a pressing cloth as well as the steam option on your iron.

5 Slip the fabric over the seat back to check it fits. It should be loose rather than snug.

6 Trace the seat shape using the same method and lining it up to the sewn back pieces. Fold the pattern paper and straighten up the pattern lines, then cut the final pattern shape and check it against the chair again. Pin the pattern to the fabric and cut one piece. Remove the slipcover back from the chair and pin the front bottom hem to the back of the seat piece, right sides together. Sew a 1cm seam, then press.

7 Measure the circumference of the chair at two points – at the seat and where you want the skirt to finish. Chair legs often 'kick-out', so you may need to make the skirt piece wider at the bottom. To create the final cutting measurement, add 2cm to the height and 8cm to the width measurements.

8 Either create a paper pattern or draw the measurements straight onto the fabric. Cut the fabric. Turn up a 1cm hem on the bottom end, press, then stitch. On the two short ends, turn 1cm to the wrong side and press. Turn over another 3cm to the wrong side on the side edges and press again. Topstitch the sides close to the edge.

9 Turn the slipcover back and seat inside out. Starting at the middle of the back, pin the skirt to the back and around the edges of the seat. When you get back to the start, the remaining short end should overlap where you started. For visual reference, think of it as a skirt with a split at the back. Sew a 1cm seam, then press.

10 Turn the slipcover right side out and slip it over the chair to check the fit. If it's looser than you would like, you can nip and tuck by sewing a wider seam allowance. I like my covers loose. I washed the cover again and left it un-pressed so that it is a truly rumpled affair and totally in keeping with the state of the chair. However, to show it a little respect, I embroidered simple Boro stitch crosses on the front of the slipcover back. You don't need a lot – about 15 minutes worth, but I think it makes all the difference.

linen pinboard

It starts with an idea

I think the simplest and most effective way to create your idea of home (or any new project) is to craft a visual record. When I was creating the overall look and feel of *Home Sewn*, I used my tried and true method – I created a mood-board. In the past I've just used large pieces of card or mountboard, but this time I wanted to make a fabric-based pinboard that would hold project plans as well as on-going inspiration.

I think high-street pinboards are too diddy – thus ensuring creativity is stifled before you even get started. A bit of research revealed that I could buy cork on a roll, which also fitted a standard cut of mdf, and – well – this pinboard was just meant to be. I already had this wonderful stash of antique linen that I knew I wanted to use across lots of the designs in *Home Sewn* and I'm handy with a staple gun, so, as they say, 'the job's a good-un'.

To create a great visual board, gather magazine images, paint charts, ephemera, fabric and – well anything really that 'speaks' to you. Once gathered, pin it all to the board to tell a story. And when the story is pinned and therefore coloured-in rather than just outlined, it makes all your choices much easier.

Shall we get started?

My pinboard is a very useful, but approximate 60 x 122cm. This is a super size for creating a single project vision. If you'd like more pinning space but want to keep it a simple solution, just make a series of boards this size and then hang or lean them together. This is easier than creating one large board as it is more flexible, simpler to put together and, most importantly, will fit in your car. There is nothing more depressing than having to walk home from a DIY store wrestling with an oversized sheet of mdf in a strong breeze...

You'll need:

600 x 1200mm roll of cork. I found mine at Hobbycraft but a Google search should overwhelm you with supplier options.

606 x 1220 x 9mm of mdf. Any DIY chain will have this in stock. Don't be tempted by the 18mm-thick board unless you are propping your pinboard on the floor.

700 x 1350mm (minimum) of fabric. Natural fabric with a looser weave is best.

You'll also need:

Spray glue of your choice. Make sure your option will adhere to wood. Spray glue is usually quite unpleasant so always read the label and take appropriate safety measures.

Staple gun and staples

Iron with steam option

Pins and scissors

Your pile of inspirational clippings and objet d'art

Wall mounts (if hanging from the wall)

To make:

1 Find a clear workspace – a dining table or freshly vacuumed floor will be perfect.

2 Press your fabric, using a steam option for best results. Set your fabric aside and open a window or door before the next step.

3 Lay your mdf flat – either side down is fine. Unroll the cork carefully (it has a tendency to crumble on corners) and position it on the mdf. The cork is slightly narrower than the mdf, so use a pencil to mark the corners so that you will know where to start laying down the cork.

4 Using a spray glue of your choice, spray one side of the cork roll. Do this in sections rather than all at once to give yourself enough time to be accurate with placement on the mdf.

5 Lining up the cork with your pencil marks, stick it down to the mdf. Continue spraying and sticking until the whole roll is attached. This isn't a long process, but don't rush it for speed's sake. Keep the breeze flowing in because glue is not great for us.

6 Lift the board and place the fabric right-side down and flat on your work surface. Then place the board cork-side down on the fabric. Make sure the board is both centred and aligned with the fabric (i.e. not on an angle as this distorts the fabric).

7 Starting with the first long side, pull the excess linen to the back of the board. Use the staple gun and staple the fabric to the board, keeping the fabric taut along the long side as you go. Repeat for the second long side, ensuring the fabric is tight and smooth as you staple.

8 At the first short end, fold the excess fabric in at the corners (like wrapping a present), stretch and staple. Try to avoid stapling on top of previous staples. Repeat for the second short end et voila! – your pinboard is complete. Twenty minutes tops, I think.

9 If you are mounting your board on a wall, plan the position and then fix wall mounts to the board and the wall.

Now you can start properly. Just place the images and objects anywhere to begin, then move them around, remove, add or start again. You'll come up with a composition that says so much more to you than their parts – home synergy = home love.

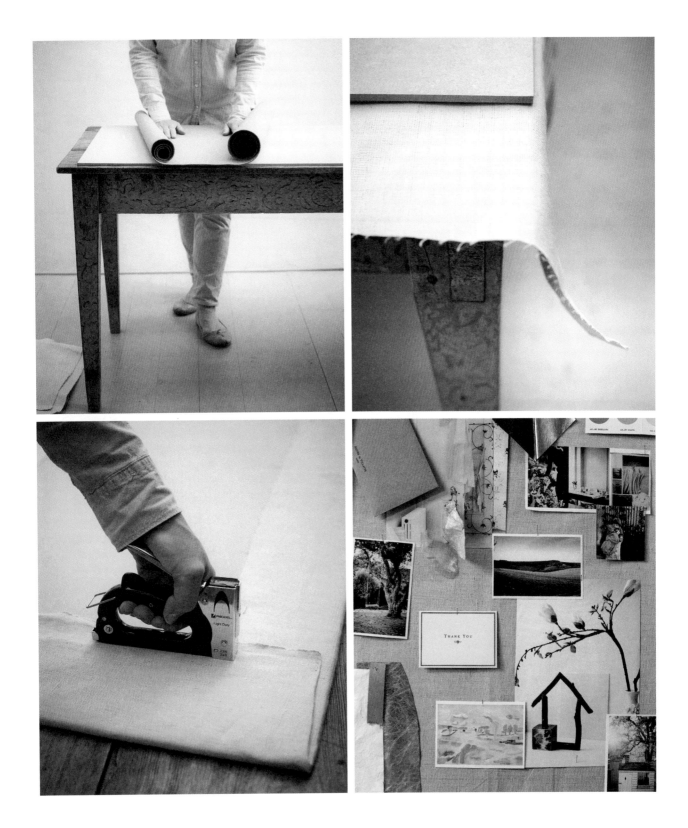

your kit

If you are an experienced maker, you will most certainly already have many, if not all, of the tools you'll need. If you're a newbie or tentatively moving from 'beginner' to 'advanced', it's not an arduous shopping experience if you are missing some bits and pieces, is it? Don't forget to check out your home tool box before you double up and it's most certainly a good idea to share out your stuff between friends and family – I'll bring the rotary cutter and you bring the hammer...

Each project lists the tools you'll need to complete them properly and safely, so check the relevant project to see what's required and why.

Sewing machine

Your sewing machine doesn't need to be expensive and it doesn't need bells and whistles for most sewing projects. Do your research to choose the right sewing machine for you. They vary in price from £49–£2000 and beyond. Most sewers use only straight or zigzag stitch, so a simple sturdy machine from a well-known manufacturer should suit. It will come with a basic selection of accessories including a standard sewing foot, needles and a bobbin or two. It's worth investing in a walking foot, zipper foot and a selection of machine needles for silk, cotton and leather.

Make sure you choose a respected brand of sewing machine, firstly because it comes with a useful warranty and, secondly, because you can find replacement parts and accessories easily. Visit a department store or local sewing centre to find a machine that you find comfortable to use and make sure you have a lesson on the machine before you take it home. Each brand has it's own quirks, so it's important to try a few. You can also buy (or borrow) excellent second-hand machines. Get your second-hand find serviced before you start sewing to make sure it is at peak performance. Google 'sewing machine service' and a good number of sewing centres and mobile service companies will pop up.

My very expensive machine broke down at a critical juncture during the writing of *Home Sewn*. Whilst it was off being repaired I made do (very well) with a very basic machine from my local department store – a good lesson for me too.

Do some research, visit a specialist shop and have a lesson. That's it really.

Needles

You'll need quilter's and embroidery needles, as well as sharps for general sewing and a darning needle for the thicker work. The packaging will describe exactly what each type of needle is and what you use them for.

Pins

You'll need:

- Dressmaking pins, extra fine and easy to use. I find long fine pins the easiest to use. Make sure they have glass or metal heads, as plastic heads will melt if they come into contact with the iron.

- Quilting pins. These are longer for working through layers of fabric.

- Entomology pins (very beautiful), or super-fine pins, for very fine fabrics.

- Safety pins.

Cutting tools

You'll need:

- Dressmaking scissors, for fabric and fabric alone. Invest well and make sure you have them regularly sharpened.

- Simple household scissors, for paper and pattern cutting.

- Thread scissors, for threads and tiny snips.

- Rotary cutter. A rotary cutter is in fact a circular razor blade, so needs to be treated with respect. You use it to cut your fabric on a cutting mat. Use it to cut fabric for quilts as it's very fast and efficient.

- Scalpel knife, for cutting leather or small/awkward items.

- Pinking shears, for zigzag edges or to finish seams.

Measuring tools

You'll need:

- Long metal ruler, between 60–90cm long, for squaring up quilts and marking long and straight lines.

- Tailor's tape measure, for extra long or shaped measuring.

- Quilter's cutting mat. A cutting mat provides a grid for you to line up your fabric. Used mostly for quilt-making, they are useful for many other projects. You can buy cutting mats in many sizes and in metric or imperial. A3 is the smallest useful size.

- Quilter's ruler. Made from transparent acrylic, these are designed to be used with cutters and mats, and they make it easy to cut fabric accurately. You'll need one that is 15 x 30cm as a minimum.

- Set square set, which can be used in place of a quilter's ruler for some projects.

From the toolbox

You'll need:

- Lightweight hammer

- Selection of domestic and artist paintbrushes

- Staple gun (make sure you take a note of the correct staple size)

- Pliers

- Awl (bradawl) – you'll find it in your toolbox, very useful for making holes.

- Masking tape, for marking quilting lines and useful for keeping fabric straight.

- Decorator's dustsheets

- Plastic decorator's gloves

- Paint cleaner for oil-based paints

- Small saw

- Leather punch, to make different-sized holes and very useful for straps, bags and purses.

Other equipment

You'll need:

- Iron with steam option for perfectly pressed seams.

- Linen or cotton pressing cloths. Use scraps of medium-weight cloth and remember they need to be damp to be effective.

- Thimbles, metal or leather. Again complete personal preference, but I use a leather one as I find it more flexible and comfortable. I have also been known to use fabric plasters when the thimble has gone walkabout, as they work well too.

- Seam ripper, for unpicking. Make sure the blade is sharp and has a comfortable handle.

- Tailor's chalk or pencil, a light and dark version of both, for marking, quilting patterns and tracing templates.

- Mechanical pencil or very sharp, hard pencils

- Soft lead pencils

- Permanent marker

- Pattern-making paper with marked gridlines

- Spray adhesive (make sure you read the instructions before using)

- Kitchen funnel and measuring jug

- Bulldog clips

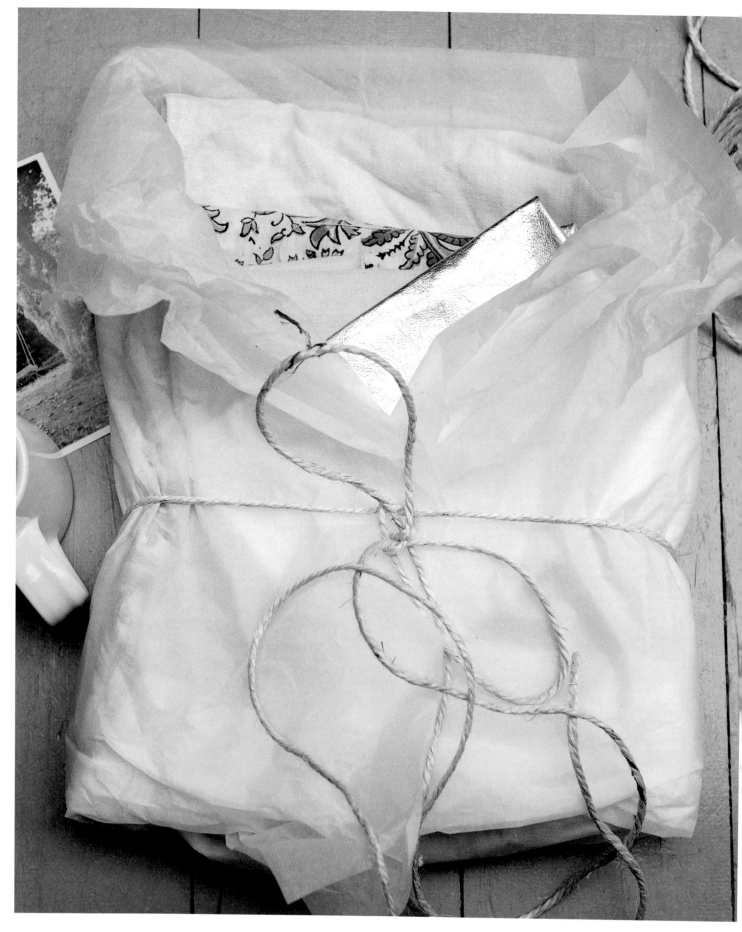

where to find your fabric and other lovely things

This list is where I bought everything for this book – retailers I've used time and again, and ones I'm always happy to return to. There are, of course, so many alternatives both online, and bricks and mortar, but I hope this is a useful start.

Fabric

CLOTH HOUSE
My go-to store for Indian block prints, linen, denim and khadi cotton, as well as their excellent cotton voile and organdie. They have fantastic silk velvets and organza, as well as a wide array of wools. They also sell a small selection of wooden blocks.

47 Berwick Street, London W1F 8SJ
www.clothhouse.com – now with online shopping

RUSSELL AND CHAPPLE
This is where you go for bulk linen and all your cotton basics. Brilliant stuff. You can shop online, but do get samples of everything first as the website doesn't show the fabric at its best.

68 Drury Lane, London WC2B 5SP
www.russellandchapple.co.uk

BECKFORD SILK
A brilliant online store for dyeable silks. They send swatches and provide a very friendly and efficient service.

www.beckfordsilk.co.uk

PARNA
Kath at Parna sources wonderful vintage linen and hemp in rolls, old sheets and more. It's excellent quality, well-curated and is the right price for what you are buying.

www.parna.co.uk

LE PREVO
If you are buying a piece or two of leather (and fittings), I think this is the best place to source from. They are helpful, will send samples and are completely happy for you to buy just one piece of leather. The purchasing process is a little old-school, but I quite like having a chat with them on the phone.

www.leprevo.co.uk

ETSY
This has been an excellent source for *Home Sewn*. Lots of great suppliers for block print and basic Indian cottons, as well as handmade waxed canvas. Do bear in mind that the actual colour of the fabric is often much brighter than the photographs. This is also the best place to buy wooden blocks online at a reasonable price.

www.etsy.com

A GREAT LONG-ARM QUILTER
My tried and trusted.

37/39 High Street, Dorking, Surrey RH4 1AR

www.quiltroom.co.uk

Or check out your local quilt shop for recommendations.

Other materials

LAMPSHADE KITS — NEEDCRAFT
For a cornucopia of lampshade kits, this is the only place you need to go. Everything is available online, combined with excellent customer service. There are instruction videos and other resource tools here too.

www.needcraft.co.uk

LEATHER — THE IDENTITY STORE
For all your leather hardware. Lovely quality and a very swift service.

www.theidentitystore.co.uk

HEADBOARD KITS
There are a good number of companies that provide headboard kits online. As I didn't use one in the end, I don't want to specify a supplier I haven't had experience of. Google 'headboard kits' to find one near you. Most sell through Ebay too. Look for a supplier that has excellent feedback, and do compare prices including the shipping costs, as this can vary hugely. After much research, I purchased the upholstery foam and wadding through a supplier on Ebay that provided great service and reasonable pricing.

FEATHER AND DOWN INNERS
I buy cushion inners in bulk, but would recommend a 'solid' department store if you want just a couple of cushions in standard sizes. Alternatively, hop on Ebay — lots of suppliers, with some who will make custom sizes.

QUILT WADDING
Again, I buy in bulk, but www.cottonpatch.co.uk is a good online source to purchase wadding in pre-cut sizes. Alternatively google 'quilt wadding' or visit your local haberdashery store. Do check the range of choice at any bricks and mortar stores before you go, as stock can be limited.

BROW FARM
This is a great resource for cherry stones and buckwheat hulls (plus numerous other fillings).

www.browfarmonlinestore.co.uk

LIQUID GILT
If you can get yourself to King's Road in Chelsea, then go to Green & Stone. It's a lovely place to shop and you'll find all manner of things.

259 Kings Road, Chelsea, London SW3 5EL
www.greenandstone.com

Otherwise Cass Art (also lovely stores) has a good selection and a number of stores around London. www.cassart.co.uk

Alternatively go online and google. (What did we do before this?)

NATURAL DYES
Of course you can use your fruit and veg, but if you want to try powdered natural dyes, try these.

www.wildcolours.co.uk

PATTERN-MAKING PAPER
For 5–10m of paper on a roll, hop onto Ebay for the most cost-effective and efficient resource. Buy paper with a grid or hatch pattern in metric!

CORK
What a find! Go directly to www.hobbycraft.co.uk. Two different sized rolls to choose from.

PINS, SCISSORS AND OTHER SEWING NEEDS
For useful and beautiful kit, go directly to www.merchantandmills.com. Their entomology pins are a must. You can buy all your basic kit from any haberdashery store, but it probably won't be as beautiful as from Merchant & Mills.

index

acknowledgements

I mostly have Ed to thank. *Home Sewn* was created whilst we travelled through an incredibly difficult time as a family. You remind me of what home truly is.

Thank you Cath for your extraordinary photographs. They are astonishingly beautiful.

Thank you Miranda – utterly beautiful book design.

Thank you to the team at Kyle Books. It is a very beautiful book, so thank you for giving me the team to work with, to make it such a lovely thing.